Dare to be Different

Dare to be Different

A leadership fable about transformational change in schools

Will Ryan

Crown House Publishing Limited
www.crownhouse.co.uk

First published by
Crown House Publishing Ltd
Crown Buildings, Bancyfelin, Carmarthen, Wales, SA33 5ND, UK
www.crownhouse.co.uk
and
Crown House Publishing Company LLC
PO Box 2223, Williston, VT 05495, USA
www.crownhousepublishing.com

Cover image © zaieiunewborn59 – fotolia.com, images pp. 55–56 © baphotte –
fotolia.com, images pp. 102–103 © NLshop – fotolia.com

The extract on p. 70 from *The Happy Manifesto: Make Your Organization a Great
Workplace* © Henry Stewart, 2013 is reproduced with the permission of Kogan Page.

British Library of Cataloguing-in-Publication Data
A catalogue entry for this book is available from the British Library.

Edited by Fiona Spencer Thomas.

Print ISBN 978-178583276-5
Mobi ISBN 978-178583280-2
ePub ISBN 978-178583281-9
ePDF ISBN 978-178583282-6

LCCN 2017951348
Printed and bound in the UK by TJ International, Padstow, Cornwall

Acknowledgements

This book is dedicated to those brilliant teachers who dare to be different and whose pupils develop a love of learning while making brilliant progress.

I would especially like to thank the following schools who have been kind enough to allow me to work with them on a regular basis and whose work has helped to shape this book:

Dinnington Community Primary School, Rotherham
Leavesden Green Primary School, Hertfordshire
Mildmay Infant School, Chelmsford
Ordsall Primary School, Retford
St Alban's Catholic Primary School, Doncaster
St Bede's Catholic Primary School, Rotherham
St Joseph's Catholic Primary School, Dewsbury
Thorpe Hesley Primary School, Rotherham
Woodthorpe Community Primary School, Sheffield

Foreword
by James Kilner

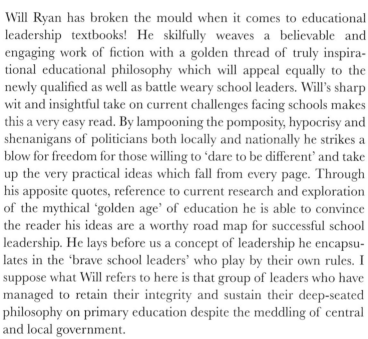

Will Ryan has broken the mould when it comes to educational leadership textbooks! He skilfully weaves a believable and engaging work of fiction with a golden thread of truly inspirational educational philosophy which will appeal equally to the newly qualified as well as battle weary school leaders. Will's sharp wit and insightful take on current challenges facing schools makes this a very easy read. By lampooning the pomposity, hypocrisy and shenanigans of politicians both locally and nationally he strikes a blow for freedom for those willing to 'dare to be different' and take up the very practical ideas which fall from every page. Through his apposite quotes, reference to current research and exploration of the mythical 'golden age' of education he is able to convince the reader his ideas are a worthy road map for successful school leadership. He lays before us a concept of leadership he encapsulates in the 'brave school leaders' who play by their own rules. I suppose what Will refers to here is that group of leaders who have managed to retain their integrity and sustain their deep-seated philosophy on primary education despite the meddling of central and local government.

I have known Will Ryan for practically the whole of his time in the world of education. It comes as no surprise to me that he is able to articulate his own deep-seated philosophy on primary education since his work as a classroom teacher – and later as a school leader and education adviser – always put enjoyment at the forefront.

As a teacher he honed his skills well working in local authorities and with teachers and leaders who were fully committed to 'the West Riding philosophy' which brightened the lives of so many children. It was a philosophy promoted by the legendary Sir Alec Clegg (CEO of the West Riding of Yorkshire from 1945 to 1974). It enriched the lives of children growing up in south and west Yorkshire from the

1950s right up until the first 'raspberry ripple' *Curriculum Matters* booklets published as Margaret Thatcher's Tory government was preparing the ground for the 1988 Education Reform Act, which was to impose the national curriculum on schools.

I remember accompanying Will on a visit to Alderley Edge in the mid 1970s as part of our class study of *The Weirdstone of Brisingamen* by Alan Garner. Well before health and safety Will and I crammed together in the caves of Alderley Edge with fifty-three Year 6 pupils (J4 in old money) and read extracts from the book describing the sleeping knights under the hills. I still meet men and women in their fifties who remember that day and that experience and how, for some, it brought reading alive for them in every sense.

Over the course of the book Will provides the reader with a rich bounty of ideas for enriching children's learning which he draws from the inspiration he gives to schools as he invents the crafty twists and turns of a vibrant curriculum with which to hook the imaginations of today's children.

Will takes us through an inspirational curriculum through the eyes and experiences of an inspirational head teacher, Brian Smith, and his various friends and foes. The villains of the piece; Roger Stonehouse, a chair of governors and leader of the council who bullies his way to power; the inept secretary of state, Rupert Brinton; and the head of Ofsted, Sir Compton Urquhart, are a compilation of so many who have held those offices in recent years.

Brian's allies are the inspirational Tom Featherstone, a local authority adviser, together with Andrea and Eve who keep Brian focused and motivated and ensure he keeps believing in himself.

The battle lines are drawn and Will successfully convinces the reader that Brian's vision will conquer the dull and lacklustre curriculum facing schools.

Within the first few pages we see Will's simple ideas of teaching three-generational lessons within a fourth-generation curriculum. The reader is left tingling at the prospect of a Disney film leading to the type of high quality maths, design and literacy and spiritual, moral, social and cultural experiences on offer with just the right amount of encouragement and inspiration. Here, even the least confident teacher, given just the right amount of freedom, can design learning which has no boundaries.

Indeed, it is no exaggeration to say that almost every page of the book contains some nugget which causes the reader to sit back in amazement at the achievements of the various characters Will parades before us.

Will has no time for 'The Vicars of Bray' who chop and change their theories of education in a vain attempt to convince inspectors that their institutions are good or outstanding. His message is loud and clear from the outset – Will is setting before the reader a vision – backed up with specific and practical school based ideas – which can rekindle in the primary schools of this country the belief that greatness and success for our future generations can be achieved: if only the leaders at the chalkface hold fast to their beliefs in how children learn and make our schools the envy of the rest of the world.

A head teacher once said to me during a review of his large primary school in the centre of a west Yorkshire city, 'My aim for the children is simple, I want our children to become good neighbours.' Mind-blowing in its simplicity but what a world our children would create for themselves if the overwhelming majority were 'good neighbours'. As you read through Will's amazing examples and practical solutions for this ever-changing world of primary education you feel the urge to take his ideas and run with them. You know deep down that Will is capturing the reason why you went into primary education, because it is your vocation and not just a job.

It is an inspirational tale. As schools prepare themselves for the next onslaught of government initiatives, as the press continue to blame teachers for all the ills of the world, Will hands to those willing to take the challenge the opportunity to take back ownership of what happens in the classroom.

In Will's time he has seen off the barmy 'Initial Teaching Alphabet' of the 1960s, with its forty-five symbols that nobody ever really got to grips with, Fletcher Maths, SMP maths (Still Millions Puzzled), reading by osmosis and all the fads and fancies which came and went over the years. No, Will sticks to what he knows best and what is proven to work well, good old-fashioned fun learning which engages and excites the children to discover and causes parents to have to listen to 'what we did at school today' open mouthed. Above all, Will inspires teachers young, old or anywhere in-between to 'dare to be different' and get back to enjoying the job they are proud to hold as a vocation in life.

Preface

The current educational climate has become obsessed with data and the collection of evidence, so here comes my contribution. Within this text you will find:

- At least one-hundred-and-eighteen tips that are based around exciting primary practice and which should make the hairs tingle on the neck of the most wizened school inspector.
- At least forty-five significant ideas that will strengthen leadership and have the capacity to transform your school as a learning community.
- At least fifty quotations that will make you think about how our most inspirational leaders create inspirational teachers who get an inspirational response from their learners.
- Compelling pieces of evidence to demonstrate that primary school teachers are doing a fabulous job, despite what any politician or reporter from the *Daily Mail* would tell you.

I have been a very lucky man. I have now spent forty-three years going in and out of the best primary schools and classrooms in this nation, and if there is one thing I have discovered it is that these wonderful places tend to make up their own rules. It was Michael Korda who said, 'The fastest way to succeed is to look like you are playing to someone else's rules whilst quietly playing by your own.' The problem in education is that politicians and administrators have constantly been changing and making up rules, leaving behind a workforce that is committed to the children in its care but worn down by political meddling. It may be a personal view, but I seriously believe that a significant proportion of actions have been taken by politicians driven by a quest for power rather than by a deep concern for the welfare of children. Indeed, sometimes their well-being has been totally neglected. For example, in May

2016 *The Guardian* carried a story about the then mayor of London concealing a report revealing that 433 schools in the capital are in areas that exceed rules on nitrogen oxide pollution. In the same edition there was an article by Jonathan Wolff based on Bernard Williams' paper 'Politics and Moral Character'. This argued that 'the characteristics that allow politicians to rise to the top might not be the virtues we seek in those who govern us: "Lying, or at least concealment and the making of misleading statements; breaking promises; special pleading; temporary coalition with the distasteful; sacrifice of the interests of worthy persons to those of unworthy persons; and (at least if it is a sufficiently important position) coercion to blackmail."'[1]

If this is the case, then it really is time for brave school leaders everywhere to start playing by their own rules. However, this can be easier said than done. I have always been impressed by the influential leadership fables of Patrick Lencioni. I believe they have the capacity to bring about transformational change. As a consequence, I have always had a desire to write a similar leadership fable within a primary school setting, and this is it. It is the story of a primary school head teacher who listens very carefully to the things his political masters say and then sets out to achieve greatness by doing the exact opposite. While the characters in the story are all fictitious, the wonderful Tom Featherstone and the butterflies he creates (i.e. the little things that make a huge difference) are based around the work of Sir Tim Brighouse.

Those forty-three years of going in and out of wonderful classrooms while trying to make sense of constant government meddling have left me with a story I have been dying to tell. As Zora Neale Hurston said, 'There is no agony like bearing an untold story inside you.' So here comes the story. I hope it proves to be a good one, because we all love a good story. We were made for them!

Contents

Acknowledgements   *v*
Foreword by James Kilner   *vii*
Preface   *xi*

1. Begin with the end in mind   1

2. A hero in waiting   18

3. The sexy subversive   25

4. Every time I use my mobile phone I take a
    photograph of my foot   36

5. Wanted: invisible leaders – apply here   52

6. Books, not bullets, will change the world   62

7. People who moan about people who moan   68

8. Six $1.5 million words   77

9. The three signs of a miserable job   87

10. When teachers learn from each other, their future
    will be secured   93

11. The problem with fronted adverbial clauses   100

12. This is the kind of English up with which I will
    not put   111

13. Three-generational lessons within a fourth-
    generation curriculum   125

14. Leopards, peanuts and compost tip Brian over
     the hedge   135

15. This way to the nuclear bunker and other secrets   149

16. Real mathematics is based in the real world   164

17. Who wants to solve a quadratic equation anyway?   168

18. Without struggle there is no progress   182

19. The power of being true to your beliefs   186

     Endnotes   *188*
     Bibliography   *205*

Chapter 1
Begin with the end in mind

Budget 2016: Every state school in England to become an academy by 2022

Daily Mail Online, 15 March 2016

Wilferd Peterson famously told us to begin with the end in mind and 'walk with the dreamers, the believers, the courageous, the cheerful, the planners, the doers, the successful people with their heads in the clouds and their feet on the ground'. This is a leadership fable about a school and its head teacher who did just that.

Brian Smith had grown tired of wave after wave of government initiatives and meddling politicians with their vanity projects. These projects were often ill-conceived and seemed to be designed to spread fear and unrest among school leaders. This was despite the fact that Ofsted inspectors were reporting that primary schools were doing well. Brian hated this approach and he also loathed the way in which certain newspapers disparaged the wonderful young people and their dedicated teachers in the nation's schools. While Her Majesty's Chief Inspector of Schools was praising the work of primary schools, some tabloids preferred to publish distorted stories that potentially corroded the spirits of committed teachers. They seemed especially to aim their venom at leaders like Brian, driven by a moral imperative to make a difference in some of our most challenging communities by daring to be different.

Brian had certainly dared to be different. Three years earlier he reached a bold and momentous decision to listen to everything his political masters said and then achieve greatness by doing the opposite. This was simply because he considered that there was more research behind his approach. Instead of feeling demoralised by the fabrications of journalists, Brian was determined that they galvanise him into action. So, for the last three years, Brian had led Springett Lane Primary School with his head in the clouds and his feet on the ground. Wilferd Peterson also told us to begin with the end so, perversely, we will start our fable at the end.

The inspector calls

The inspection of Springett Lane Primary School had gone well. In fact, it went better than that. The inspectors witnessed some remarkable primary practice taking place within a learning community where both children and adults believed they could achieve, had a duty to achieve and had a duty to help others achieve. This was the culmination of brave and inspired leadership and, rightly, it was about to trigger much celebrating.

The inspection had taken place late in the autumn term when the whole school had become absorbed in a project entitled 'Fire and Ice', to reflect not only the winter months but also the forthcoming Winter Olympics. The school was looking spectacular. By this stage the teachers had fully embraced the concept of immersive learning environments – where learners become totally absorbed in a self-contained and stimulating environment – which may, in reality, be artificial, but to the children it is absolutely real.

Armed with their clipboards, the inspectors joined the children as they passed by the lamp post and through the old wooden wardrobe that had replaced the door to Claire's Key Stage 2 classroom, before entering the fictitious land of Narnia. The children in this class became hooked into a huge project around C. S. Lewis' classic children's novel, *The Lion, the Witch and the Wardrobe*.

Another stunning learning environment could be found in Year 5. The classroom reflected the huge success the children had achieved with their project based around that most ill-fated of British ships, the RMS *Titanic*. The work had culminated in the children running a museum for the day. Following invitations written by the pupils, the lord mayor had arrived in all his finery to open the proceedings. At the centre of the museum was a large-scale model of the liner. The displays celebrated the pupils' considerable achievements in all areas of the curriculum. Children dressed as passengers and crew members and circulated among the parents and wider community to share their information with confidence. There were PowerPoint presentations and films as the children took up the mantle of the expert, leaving visitors astonished by the youngsters' capacity to hold their audience. It was one of those rare occasions when you could reach out and touch the children's passion for learning. The school's emphasis on spoken language had paid huge dividends.

Another great success story had been in Rob's class. As a teacher, he had initially shared immense concerns when Brian had introduced the notion of teaching three-generational lessons within a fourth-generation curriculum. (If you are confused by these terms, dear reader, all will become clear in the fullness of time.) Rob feared there would be a lack of textbooks and of the structures he had become reliant upon. On more than one occasion he had sat in Brian's staff meetings saying, 'It's no good. I just don't get it!' During the Christmas holidays he had settled down in front of the television to watch a rerun of one of his favourite films. He had seen *Cool Runnings* so many times that he knew virtually every word. While watching it again, he reached out for his coffee cup and froze as he suddenly said out loud: 'Feel the rhythm! Feel the rhyme! By Jove I've got it, it's bobsleigh time!' In a flash of inspiration, he set about building a term's work around the Disney film which tells the story of the almost-true trials and tribulations of the Jamaican bobsleigh team who took part in the Calgary Winter Olympic Games in 1988.

Springett Lane Primary School had developed a unique approach to its fourth-generation curriculum, which was based around teachers taking unusual ideas and running with them and encouraging children to imagine what a better world might look like. While all this was going on, the youngsters would be learning some real, interesting and hard stuff. For Rob, *Cool Runnings* proved to be the ideal vehicle. Yes, it just happened to be his favourite child-hood film, but that was a significant advantage as it gave him huge subject knowledge.

The project was never about the children sitting and watching the DVD version of the film. Rob simply took extracts from it and told stories about what happened next. As a consequence, the children studied the climate and topography of Jamaica. They also found out about the scars slavery had left behind. In trying to establish why Jamaicans would be any good at bobsleighing, they looked at the history of cart racing on the Caribbean island and also the significance of the sprint start. It is a well-known fact that, over recent years, many of the world's best sprinters have come from Jamaica and the children duly set about researching and writing biographies of famous Jamaican sprinters.

The children became totally engrossed, but it didn't stop there. The children also examined deeper and more emotive issues. When they heard about the Jamaican team being disqualified because their bobsleigh was deemed to be rickety and old, they explored how this totally went against the Olympic ideals. From this they considered whether these principles would make a good set of classroom rules that could guide them. The film shows how athletes from other countries turned their animosity on to the Jamaican team and announced, 'This is not for you, Jamaica. Go home.' This comment was driven by racist attitudes and, as a consequence, the children started to investigate the thorny issues of racism and how it might be possible to change attitudes. The coach of the Jamaican team had previously been banned from the sport for cheating, so the learners questioned whether or not it was ever right to cheat. The infamous bobsleigh crash in the film – when the bruised and shell-shocked Jamaican team raise their sleigh onto their shoulders to carry it across the finishing line, to the applause and cheers of spectators – made the children think deeply about when they too had dug deep and demonstrated resilience to ensure they finished their own metaphorical race.

A further requirement at Springett Lane Primary School was that, at various stages, the teacher had to plan a lesson that was so exciting it stayed with the children forever. These lessons had to be so powerful that, in later life, these memorable experiences would return to the fore. Then, the former pupils would describe their magical moments at Springett Lane Primary School first to their own children and then their grandchildren. This made the lesson truly three generational.

This three-generational lesson proved to be a magical highlight for Rob's class. It took place on a crisp February morning and the day dawned cold but bright. Frost from the night before glistened on the school field as the temperature struggled to rise above freezing point. One by one, as was the procedure at Springett Lane, the teachers went out onto the playground to bring their classes into school. On this particular morning, Rob quite deliberately didn't do this. Instead, he left them outside where they remained for a further ten minutes. Then, either because they felt cold or from a sense of duty, the children decided to take themselves into school. When they arrived at their classroom they received an electrifying surprise that gave them goosebumps. In the centre of the classroom was a shiny blue bobsleigh with the union flag emblazoned on it. If a gasp can be audibly silent, then that was the impact of this spectacular sight!

The next person to come into the room was wearing a Great Britain tracksuit. She was called Nicola. She looked at the youngsters and announced, 'Good morning children, I have come to tell you my story.' She went on to tell them that when she had been at primary school and sports day came around, she was entered for a race called the fifty-yard dash. Having felt totally deflated when she finished in last place, she decided that practice was the order of the day. Over the following days, weeks and months, she went away and trained and trained and trained. But the gains were only marginal, as the following year she finished next to last. Clearly some progress had been made but further training was called for, and this led to further gains as the following year she finished third to last. However, by this stage Nicola had started to enjoy running and had joined an athletics club. Over time she ran in many races, but in the big races that really mattered she could only ever finish as a runner-up. As a keen sportsperson desperate for success, she then decided that drastic action was called for and decided to change sport. At the suggestion of her coach, Nicola took up bobsleighing. It was reasoned that her strong sprint starts would be a great asset in her new bobsleigh racing career.

At this point Nicola stopped speaking and sat the children in teams of four staring up at a giant screen where a computer-generated bobsleighing animation was ready to run. She went on to explain to the children that she wanted them to understand what it felt like to go down an icy bobsleigh track at speeds approaching 100 miles per hour. The film started to roll. In perfect synchronisation, the children swayed left or right to go through the bends, with each member of the team matching the movements of their leader because they knew they had to remain aerodynamic. Some children had a sense of fear in their eyes and tightly gripped the waist of the person in front of them. They cheered as the bobsleigh finally crossed the finishing line.

Nicola then continued to tell her story. Upon entering her first ever bobsleigh race (and I guess you have worked out the outcome) she came last. So, as was the case previously, she went away and practised, practised, practised, only to finish second to last in her next race. However, through grit and determination she made progress. Finally she said to the children, 'Now I want to show you a film from the bobsleigh world championships.'

The film started with Nicola leaping into the bobsleigh with her race partner. It then showed the sleigh speeding and swaying around the bends at breakneck speed. The children cheered when the green light came on because this meant that Nicola's bobsleigh was in the lead. Collectively they shouted 'Faster!' when the red light came on because this meant greater speed was needed if the championship was to be won. As they passed the finishing line and the two athletes leapt from the bobsleigh to punch the air and celebrate their victory, the children turned away from the screen and looked at Nicola who simply reached into her bag and pulled out the gold medal. The bright sunlight on that clear morning struck the medal and it seemed to dance in front of their eyes.

After the Ofsted inspector had spoken to the children – or, more accurately, noted down their sheer joy and passion – she simply wrote in the inspection report, 'Pupils are excited to meet accomplished sports people such as the bobsleigh world champion.'[1]

As the lesson came to a close and the children reflected on the huge range of things they had learned during the lesson, one of the children looked up and said to Rob, 'Sir, you are the coolest teacher ever.' Afterwards, Rob pondered on what had made him worthy of such an accolade. He had certainly become aware of the power of using popular culture through a visual literacy approach. However, what he hadn't known at that point was that his classroom would become a hub of excellence within the school for promoting popular culture and visual literacy as a tool for high quality learning.

Springett Lane had successfully created its own teaching school within its four walls. This had been achieved through talented and passionate teachers developing their classrooms as hubs of excellence for key elements of the school's work. These hubs were used to inspire and provide training for others. They were more about promoting an approach to teaching rather than subject or academic content. For Brian Smith, it was as much about how you teach it as what it is you teach.

Many inspirational teachers will have harnessed the power of a 'wow start' in the form of a mysterious, and usually fictitious, letter which arrives at the school. In the early years foundation stage, a letter from the king may arrive on a velvet cushion asking for the help of the children. Further up the school, it may arrive in a brown business-like envelope stating that part of the school field is going to be compulsorily purchased in order for a supermarket to be built. But in Karen and David's job-share class, it arrived in a Basildon Bond white envelope with the address written in the most beautiful handwriting from a gentleman who desperately wanted the support of the children. For those readers and teachers who are interested in the 'beg, steal or borrow' approach, here is a transcript of the letter:

> 19 Sea View
> Bridlington, East Yorkshire
>
> Dear Headmaster,
>
> I am writing to you using my best handwriting. I learned to write like this at your school in the 1960s. I have never written to a headmaster before and I am worried because I was never any good at English. I was much better at shillings and pence and feet and inches.
>
> I often got into trouble at school. As I grew up I had a very good friend called Charlie. We played together and often got into trouble. We were together until the J3 class. Then one November morning Charlie dropped a bombshell. He and his family were moving to Australia. They only paid £10. I think they went on a ship. I dread to think how long that took. Anyway, all I really knew was that my best mate would soon be gone. Can you imagine how that felt?
>
> Before Charlie left we were both upset. You should have seen us crying. I remember that Charlie left the area on 15 December. I have not seen him from that day to this.

Before we parted we decided to do a really strange thing. We had both bought Christmas presents for each other but we never exchanged them. Instead, we hid them away in an old brown box along with some other things that were special to us. We made a pledge to each other that we would share the presents on the day we met again ... but we never did meet again, and now nearly fifty years have passed.

Now the strange thing is, last week I heard from Charlie and he wants to come and see me, and if it is at all possible I would like to find that box. We hid it deep in a corner of a school stockroom because we didn't want the teachers to find us with it, and I can't help wondering if it is still there.

I can't remember what present I bought for Charlie, but I know it was a popular toy at the time. It will only have cost a few bob and certainly not more than three and a tanner. I think we put some money in the box so we could buy some Spangles from Gowers and Burgons, and go and watch our favourite football team or even go and watch a Norman Wisdom film at the local Essoldo.

If somebody could look for our box it would make me very happy, because when Charlie and I meet up we would finally be able to exchange our Christmas presents. It is only a thought but maybe we could even come to school to do this.

I hope I have given you enough information, but if not you could always email me. My email address is grandpajoe@netcom.co.uk.

Thank you. I am glad I haven't made any blots. I used to get the cane for that in the old days.

Yours sincerely,
Joe Hemmings

While the information in the letter was not true, it was based around an event that could have really happened. Not surprisingly, the first thing the children did was to go off and search for the cardboard box. Now, given that the letter was a fabrication, it may or may not surprise you to find out that the box was finally located and lifted down from a shelf. It was covered in fifty years of dust. Just as the letter indicated, it was filled with a treasure trove of souvenirs from the 1960s, including a range of replica toys which are increasingly available to purchase these days. The children immediately set about emailing Grandpa Joe with the good news. However, this was only the beginning as much more was to follow.

In the letter that Karen and David had composed, they had skilfully created lines of investigation that hooked in the children. The learners did find out how and why you could go to Australia for £10. They worked out how long the journey would have taken and also where the boat would have stopped. They found out about feet and inches, shillings and pence and Norman Wisdom. After each successful line of enquiry they emailed Grandpa Joe with their findings. The children never knew that the emails were simply going through to Karen and David's computers. They read the children's research with glee before sending out a new set of emails which would trigger further research.

As Christmas drew near, Karen and David found a suitable person to play the role of Grandpa Joe. They carefully picked someone with a drama background who would have the skills to make the story believable. With all the appropriate internet safety checks in place, the children now started FaceTime communication with Grandpa Joe. Because of the way in which the school had encouraged children to talk about their learning, they were bursting with enthusiasm as they eagerly passed on information about events from the 1960s, such as the shooting of John F. Kennedy, the first episode of *Doctor Who* and Martin Luther King's role in the Civil Rights Movement.

The project was heading towards a superb finale because Charlie had now returned from Australia and was scheduled to meet his long lost childhood friend at the school on 15 December. This would be the day of the three-generational lesson which would live with the children forever more when the men finally exchanged the Christmas presents they had bought for each other fifty years earlier.

This special day came after the inspectors had been and gone. Many of the country's hardened inspectors believe they should never smile, in case it is seen as a sign of approval. Maybe if they had been there with their stern faces and clipboards, even they might have shed an emotional tear.

A local actor (and drama adviser) called Mick was standing in the school entrance when a somewhat rotund and aggressive parent jabbed her finger at him and said, 'Are you Grandpa Joe? Because if you are, I'm sick and tired of hearing about you!' He was indeed Grandpa Joe and he was about to be shepherded into the hall because the whole school had now gathered in anticipation of seeing two former pupils, now in their sixties, finally exchange their festive gifts in front of 300 children who felt they were experiencing the true spirit of Christmas.

Jonathan Smith once wrote that as a teacher you are an actor, parent, director and improviser, but 'it's not so much a Hollywood epic as a low-budget movie with a hand-held camera'.[2] This seemed to sum up what happened next which was orchestrated with precision timing. Karen and David escorted Grandpa Joe into the hall. There was no sign of Charlie anywhere. The children sang 'In the Bleak Midwinter', dwelling on the key words with genuine feeling. There was still no sign of Charlie, but there was nevertheless a hope that he would turn up before long. After a reading from the scriptures about the gifts that were given to the infant Jesus, there was poignant anticipation in the air. However, Charlie had still not made an appearance. After a short period of quiet and spiritual reflection, it was becoming clear that Charlie would not make it, and with heavy hearts the children duly stood ready to return to their classrooms. Their disappointment was weighing heavily when the hall doors flew open and in strode Charlie. His role was being played by a retired member of her majesty's inspectorate who was desperate to join in the project because he believed that this kind of work should be at the heart of the primary curriculum. As the Christmas presents were finally exchanged in front of the 300 hushed children, even the toughest of the tough had a tear of joy trickling down their cheek.

After the children had returned to their classrooms, they donned their tie-dye t-shirts and demonstrated to Charlie and Grandpa Joe how they could do the twist. Then they played with yo-yos before sitting down with them to watch Norman Wisdom moving from one disaster to another while rattling down the street in a horse-drawn milk cart. After the inspector found out about the story of Grandpa Joe, along with other evidence she had collected, she wrote: 'The curriculum is planned well and provides positive experiences that

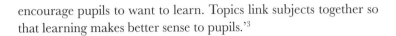

encourage pupils to want to learn. Topics link subjects together so that learning makes better sense to pupils.'[3]

Tales from Old Nan's fireside

During the three years prior to the inspection, the school had placed an emphasis on the children developing an understanding of their local community, both past and present. Studying local history was viewed as crucial in giving the children a sense of identity through exploring their heritage, and nobody did it better than 'Old Nan'. You wouldn't have thought it possible to get thirty children into her front parlour, but at various stages during the term thirty children had made the short walk through the wintery streets to listen to Old Nan's tales by her fireside. On each occasion, she sat by the glowing coals and told stories about the community from times gone by. As an octogenarian, she had a wealth of local anecdotes from her own life, but she also had other tales from her father and grandfather. The children sat wide eyed as she told them about the 'Bag Muck Strike' at the local colliery. She described with clarity the day 200 mounted police officers had moved into the area to start evicting miners and their families from their homes as the strike progressed into a second month. She read from a contemporary newspaper to tell the children that 'Snow had fallen the previous night and to add to the pitiableness of the scene, the rain fell in icy torrents during most of the time the evictions were being carried out and women and little children drenched to the skin could be seen huddled together at the roadside unable to find any shelter.' The newspaper showed photographs of furniture being lifted through windows, overladen carts and row upon row of tents as the miners set up makeshift homes on open wasteland. The photographs bore a striking resemblance to a twenty-first century refugee camp.

The debates about who was right or wrong in the Bag Muck Strike raged long and hard. What we do know is that it was difficult to mine the coal, which was extracted by hand, and for every bag of coal the miners bagged they had to bag a pile of muck. The miners only got paid for the coal, and this seemed unfair to them.

On other occasions Old Nan spoke of the locals who had fought and died in the world wars and of those who were awarded medals for bravery. On a lighter note, she spoke of queuing at the local cinema, the opening of the first supermarket and collecting Green Shield Stamps. Each visit opened up the start of a new and rich learning journey.

Chocolate and mathematics

Paul Dirac said that God used beautiful mathematics in creating the world. Over the following years, Brian – with the assistance of his loyal subject leader, Margaret – had worked to ensure that teachers and children celebrated both the beauty and creativity of mathematics. Margaret had developed her classroom into a hub of excellence and she too blew the inspectors away with the quality of her mathematical teaching.

Edsger Dijkstra reportedly declared that there should be no such thing as boring mathematics, but for Margaret's class there wasn't enough time to become absorbed in quotations as they were far too busy resolving other issues which required them to harness the power of maths. The children had found Professor Arthur Johnson's old and battered briefcase at the local bus stop. Of course, they hadn't realised whose bag it was at this stage. This information had only emerged later after a lengthy conversation about what they should do with the briefcase in case it was a suspect package. Eventually, after the children agreed to contact the police, a local community support officer duly appeared and opened the case to reveal a large number of chocolate bars, including cheaper supermarket own brands and examples of Christmas confectionery. Also in the bag was a notebook including Professor Johnson's contact details at the Department for Consumer Affairs and letters from a well-known consumer magazine and a filmmaker.

The children read the letters with care and then examined Professor Johnson's notebook. The letters read:

Dear Professor Johnson,

I would like to thank you and your team of experts for agreeing to carry out a consumer test into which chocolate bars offer the best value for money. As discussed, you are allowed to use your own criteria for this project. Additionally, we would like to know if festive chocolate products offer good value for money at this time of year.

We hope that the samples and the price lists we have provided help the process.

We would especially be interested to know if any ethical issues affect the outcomes of your research. Here is a link you might find helpful: www.bbc.co.uk/news/world-africa-15686731.

Unfortunately, there is a very short timescale for this work and it needs to be received into our offices by noon tomorrow.

Yours sincerely,

A. Cash

Consumer News Magazine

Dear Professor Johnson,

Our film company understands that you have been commissioned by Consumer News Magazine to carry out a survey into which chocolate bars offer the best value for money.

We would be grateful if you could make a one-minute film outlining the key findings of your work. However, we would need to receive your film by noon tomorrow.

We look forward to your contribution.

Yours sincerely,

Annie Mation

Commissioning Director

One-Minute Films Ltd

After reading the letters it was quickly agreed that a phone call should be made to Professor Johnson. Strangely, the call went straight through to Margaret's husband who simply pretended to be the forgetful professor. Within no time, the children moved into teams of six who were commissioned to carry out the chocolate survey and make the film. The children made calculations using cost, weight, taste and cocoa content. The internet link provided in the letter explored significant ethical issues, including the illegal use of child labour in the cocoa industry. The clip showed children as young as 10 with wounds from the machetes they used to cut the cocoa pods, while others were spraying the plants with dangerous pesticides. At this stage, the children realised there were other issues involved in establishing the true price of a bar of chocolate.

The children then researched the significance of Fairtrade and found out about the work of the Rainforest Alliance. They developed an understanding of how these organisations work to improve the labour and living conditions for cocoa farmers. The children's research took them into those complex issues that the world desperately needs to resolve. New technologies were used throughout the process to enhance the learning. The inspection team loved the activity and noted that it was highly successful because of previous opportunities where the children had carried out consumer tests in this way.

The other Year 4 class also undertook a consumer survey based around popular culture. Their project was to analyse the mathematics behind football sticker albums. They duly purchased an album which required over 300 stickers to complete. They also bought twenty packets of five stickers at 50 pence each, then checked how many repeat stickers had materialised. They went on to discover that it would probably take a four-figure sum to complete the album.

The inspectors also saw Margaret's influence in another class where the children were working out if a one penny coin could ever be worth more than a £20 note. Initially, the pupils debated whether the metal that made up the coin was more valuable than the paper. It was also accepted that the coin was more durable, and one child said that her father frequently left bank notes in the pockets of his clothes when he filled the washing machine. Another boy told the story of a very old football programme he owned which dated back to the 1950s. It came from a match his great-grandfather had played in. The game had ended in tragedy: his grandfather's leg was badly broken, and although he was rushed to hospital, nothing could be done to save the leg and it had to be amputated. The cost of the programme was just three old pennies. The boy went on to say he would never sell that football programme, not even for £300. The mood in the classroom became subdued as the children realised that some things had very little material value but huge personal value.

Margaret grasped this moment to introduce a version of the bible story of the widow's mite, which she had carefully adapted. The story told of Jesus and his followers in the temple at a time when people were expected to give money to the poor. Jesus asked those gathered around him to watch how people were putting money into the collection box. Margaret's story went on to describe how one rich merchant who owned 1,000 gold coins waited until he could be the centre of attention. He walked forward in his golden cloak and with a flourish gave away one gold coin for every one he owned. Next a trader came forward who also owned 1,000 gold coins, but he looked really miserable as he put 100 of them into the collection box. The third person in the story was the king who had great wealth because he taxed the people heavily. He loudly announced that he would donate half of his 10,000 gold coins, and then challenged everybody else to do the same. Margaret's story described how there was then a long pause in the proceedings until an elderly widow walked forward and placed two small coins called mites into the collection box. Those who watched on made disapproving tutting noises, but Jesus announced that she had given more than anyone else. At the end of the story, the children went on to rank who had been the most and the least generous, but they had to justify their answers mathematically. The perceptive learners quickly focused on fractions and percentages rather than the number of coins. At a later stage, the children learned about how many of the major religions require their followers to give a proportion of their wealth to those who are more needy.

The Year 3 class were investigating some of the beautiful patterns in numbers by adding three consecutive numbers. A range of patterns materialised but the children were especially intrigued by the fact that when the three consecutive numbers were added you always arrived at a multiple of three. The children's curiosity grew further when they discovered that when you added up the digits that make up any multiple of three you would get another multiple of three. However, the children were disappointed to discover that if you add four consecutive numbers you don't get a multiple of four. When they added five consecutive numbers they found another range of patterns, and this told them that mathematics was indeed beautiful. It was at the point where the children discovered that if you add three consecutive numbers that the digital root would be 3, 6 or 9 that the inspector scurried from the room in order to find a mathematical dictionary!

Enterprise education had been a key driver in the school's approach to teaching mathematics. The children regularly developed their own mini-businesses. Any funds raised by the young entrepreneurs went to a range of charities. Each year group worked with a different type of charity, and in addition to raising much needed funds the children found out about that particular organisation's good deeds. During the inspection, the school council presented the accounts from all the mini-businesses and spoke at length about the mathematics behind their work, outlining how much money had been raised for good causes through their desire to make a difference.

Speaking of making a difference, a significant factor in planning those memorable lessons that will remain with the children forever was to consider how they might feel, as we also know that youngsters have a burning desire to create a better and fairer world. The inspectors noted the power of this work when they reported that the school had won an international global award and had communicated with children in South Africa during the process. They said:

> Through a series of well-planned lessons and visits, the pupils are well prepared for life in modern Britain, developing an understanding of cultures and families that are different to their own. Some pupils are members of a human rights group and spoke to their Member of Parliament about local issues. One pupil won a competition to meet the Prime Minister in Downing Street. She asked him what he thought life would be like in the North of England in ten years' time. Leaders and teachers have made full use of these experiences to help the pupils learn about the democratic process.[4]

The school's focus on outdoor learning was also highly evident during the inspection. In the corridors and classrooms there was evidence that the children were working outdoors because the staff at Springett Lane believed memorable experiences led to memorable learning. The children responsible for the school weather station recorded that temperatures fell below freezing point. The Year 2 class completed a sensory trail along the school's adopted footpath, stopping to break the ice on puddles and put their hands in the frost before returning to the classroom to produce descriptive writing of genuine quality. They left food outside for the birds and recorded the different species that visited the bird table. Nobody was going to say that they were suffering from the twenty-first century condition of 'nature-deficit disorder'.[5]

The government hits reverse gear

Brian had undoubtedly achieved great success. With the help of research and other people, he had created a school that was unique, special and capable of transforming the life chances of young people. He stood resolute against so many of the government's short term plans. Inspection frameworks had come and gone, as had government agencies, curricular guidance and assessment criteria. Many of these plans had been ill-conceived. Within two months of the government announcing their plans to raise educational standards by turning all schools into academies and defiantly promising there was 'no reverse gear' in this process, the plans were thrown into the dustbin and even the *Daily Mail* accused the government of having chaotic education policies.[6]

Brian Smith stood firm against these chaotic policies. The *Daily Mail*'s insults and disparaging comments came regularly, but instead of eroding his spirits they merely added to his resolve. In short, the head teacher of Springett Lane Primary School decided to leave the politicians and journalists behind. He was on a different journey. He would walk with the dreamers and the believers, the courageous and the cheerful, the planners and the doers – and he would certainly leave Springett Lane a far better place than he found it. This is his story.

Chapter 2
A hero in waiting

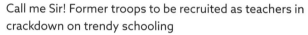

Call me Sir! Former troops to be recruited as teachers in crackdown on trendy schooling

Daily Mail Online, 24 November 2010

Brian Smith was a good head teacher. No, he was better than that – he was a really good head teacher. But he wasn't a great head teacher. Well, not yet – that would follow in the course of time. He was certainly passionate about his work and constantly sought to improve. He thought deeply and read widely because he liked to find new approaches. He firmly believed in that wise old saying, 'If you always do what you've always done, you always get what you've always got,' and that was the last thing the children who lived in the deprivation cycle that existed on the estate around Springett Lane Primary School needed. These kids didn't just need education, they needed inspiration and aspiration. At the point where the three came together there would be real hope for them.

By and large the system had failed these young people, year in, year out. Social mobility in the area was only marginally better than it was in the 1970s. The political jargon referred to the estate of inter-war, pebble-dashed, semi-detached houses as a 'lower layer super output area', which is defined as a locality that includes the most deprived postcodes in the country. It is a most bizarre term: the estate could never be described as super and any measurable positive output was minimal. There were several streets where no adults held any formal qualifications and too many young people were in neither employment nor training after finishing full time education.

Councillor Roger Stonehouse was both the chair of governors and leader of the council. He was often rude and abrupt. Others described him as a bully. He had grudgingly welcomed Brian to the school two-and-a-half years ago and immediately pointed out that this was the estate where all the worst thieves lived. He followed this up with, 'and they are only the worst thieves because they keep getting caught and that's because they are thick'. Clearly he did not have much empathy with the community. At the time of the headship interviews, Roger Stonehouse had not supported Brian's appointment; he had an alternative preferred candidate but was out-voted as democracy took its course. He thought Brian's ideas were too trendy. He had commented, 'He will amount to nowt with all his reading and posh words.' The chair of governors did much stamping of feet and there was some use of indecorous language, because this was the strategy he regularly used to get his own way. However, on this occasion it failed. The other governors, with the support of Tom Featherstone, the adviser for the local authority, voted for Brian. After the selection process had been completed, Roger Stonehouse had pushed Tom against the wall and told him to keep his nose out in future. An additional word was placed in front of the word 'nose' but this has been omitted in order to protect the sensitivity of those reading this tale.

There had been numerous complaints about Councillor Stonehouse over the years, but he made sure they had been hushed up and filed away by loyal, frightened or bullied council employees. Those who crossed him did not tend to survive long and sadly that included Tom. Roger Stonehouse had well and truly marked his card.

There was some truth in Roger Stonehouse's description of Springett Lane Primary School. It *was* in the middle of a difficult and challenging estate, and just last week Brian had arrived at school to see the words 'Smithy is scum!' painted across the wall. He was, however, especially pleased to note the correct use of the capital letter and an exclamation mark.

Brian wanted to bring about change for the children and the community he served. He knew it was a significant challenge against uneven odds, but he also knew that the sense of failure would never hurt as much as a feeling of regret. For this reason, Brian had built up an extensive collection of educational texts which allowed him to look at educational issues from a range of perspectives and not merely respond to government rhetoric or initiatives. However, he had also developed a very strange habit of trawling the internet to collect ridiculous headlines from the *Daily Mail* relating to schools and teachers. At the start he didn't know why he did it. He just did. Originally, Brian had wondered if this was an early sign of madness, but over time he started to realise what underpinned this peculiar activity.

The media and politicians seemed obsessed with running down the education system. Brian knew that this could sap parental good-will and also deter many of the best young minds from becoming teachers. He stockpiled the headlines because they made him angry, and that anger motivated and spurred him into action. At a time of life when some of his colleagues of a similar age were slowing down and contemplating retirement and cut-price September cruises, a quick glance at the *Daily Mail* headlines reinvigorated him and drove him forward.

Now, to pump further adrenalin into Brian's veins, there was a new kid on the block in the form of the Right Honourable Rupert Brinton, the new secretary of state for education. He, along with reporters from tabloid newspapers, struggled to say anything posi-tive about schools, school leaders or teachers who regularly worked in excess of seventy hours a week in a job from which it is impossible to switch off. In many ways this was strange, given the fact that in each year between 2014 and 2016 Ofsted offered glowing praise when reporting on the state of primary schools. In Her Majesty's Chief Inspector's report into England's schools in 2015, 88% of parents stated that they would recommend their child's primary school to another parent and 85% of young people were attending a primary school graded good or better by the inspectorate.[1] By 2016, Ofsted noted that the education of children under the age of 11 had never been better.[2] However, sadly this didn't make the news because in this nation, the policy of the press and powers that be is to deride rather than praise teachers.

Somebody once famously said that if you stand still for long enough you become a radical, and that certainly seemed to be the case with Rupert Brinton who firmly believed that the duty of a teacher was to impart knowledge authoritatively and with a firm sense of discipline to pupils smartly dressed in crisp blazers. Before moving into government, he had written in *The Times* that, as an educationalist, he was a traditionalist and believed that chil-dren learned best sitting in rows, knowing the kings and queens of England and reciting poetry.[3] There is an old Hebrew proverb which says, 'Do not confine your children to your own learning, for they were born in another time.' Potentially that was what Rupert Brinton was doing through the opinions he espoused on teaching and learning, and that was why he was a radical rather than a traditionalist.

On other occasions, the head of Ofsted, Sir Compton Urquhart, joined in and set about disparaging teachers in the popular press. In the past, he had alienated teachers when he changed the definition of satisfactory from 'providing satisfaction' to 'requiring improvement'.[4] This had caused considerable unrest across the teaching profession. Rupert Brinton also managed, very quickly, to fall out with the nation's teachers and provoke a similar negativity. Maybe it came from the lukewarm response to his suggestion that schoolchildren should help raise funds to contribute to a new royal yacht. Equally, his gift of a King James Bible with a personal dedication for every school had not necessarily been received with gushing gratitude, especially in schools where significant numbers of pupils don't follow the Christian faith.[5]

The *Daily Mail* and the Rupert Brinton factor

One of the *Daily Mail* headlines in Brian's collection was, 'Call me Sir! Former troops to be recruited as teachers in crackdown on trendy schooling'. This headline truly annoyed Brian. First, it implied that the discipline of young people was a problem in many schools within challenging communities. Behaviour was certainly not a problem at Springett Lane. Teachers did not confront the youngsters like an aggressive sergeant major. They sought to raise the esteem and aspiration of those in their care by catching them being good, attentive scholars and making sure positive exchanges outnumbered negative ones by at least three to one. Brian had teachers in his school who knew that if they went into conflict mode with children, there would only be one winner – and it wouldn't be them. It seemed that Brian's approach was replicated elsewhere as inspectors reported that they 'rarely observe very poor behaviour in primary schools'.[6]

While the comments of the inspectors were glowing, the *Daily Mail* ran fifteen articles criticising behaviour in schools between 2012 and 2015. However, there was a second element to this particular headline which was deeply worrying, and that was the derogatory comment about trendy schooling. Brian passionately believed the nation needed schools that were prepared to do things differently. Every truly successful business has a research unit which allows them to develop new ways of working, but how many of England's schools fulfil that ideal? Brian wanted to lead a school that dared to do things differently and genuinely broke the mould. Indeed, it was the only way forward in a community like Springett Lane.

Brian despised the journalists who were responsible for such headlines. He considered that they knew nothing about life around Springett Lane. Statistically he was correct. Over half of Britain's best paid journalists are educated in private schools, compared to one out of fourteen people nationally, and that hardly equipped them to have a deep understanding of the nation's most challenging communities. Furthermore, the annual Ipsos MORI Veracity Index indicated that journalists were employed in one of the least trustworthy professions in the land. Their ranking was similar to that of estate agents. The only good news was that there were two professions that performed even worse than them.[7]

A chumocracy

Rupert Brinton had done well for himself politically. Unlike many in the cabinet he had not been to Eton. The prime minister, a man who liked to be called Andy because he considered himself to be a man of the people, seemed to surround himself with other chaps who wore the old Etonian school tie. Rupert Brinton clearly did not fit this bill. Some people had the audacity to challenge Andy about the way in which he gave precedence to his former schoolmates, but he retorted that they couldn't be his old school pals because they had attended the school at different times to him, and anyway they were the best people for the job. Not everybody saw it that way. Some said he was running a 'chumocracy'.[8]

From the moment of his elevation to secretary of state for education, Rupert Brinton was keen to portray an image of traditionalism. In the entrance to his offices, he replaced the photographs of happy, smiling children learning in rich environments using a range of new technologies with an antique wooden school desk complete with inkwell.[9] With this one act he associated learning with drudgery. The secretary of state deemed that his classical education as a child had equipped him well. However, others thought that he was out of touch with the reality of working in challenging communities, the schools that served them and childhood in particular. The latter may be an unfair criticism. In fairness to Rupert Brinton, he did have certain child-like qualities. He especially liked to participate in a bit of name-calling. Sometimes it was posh name-calling – he frequently referred to those who were against his plans as 'Trotsky-ites'. Sometimes it was name-calling of a more puerile variety. He called a group of academics whose research suggested that some of his ideas were misjudged, 'The Blob'.[10] However, few would doubt that he was a determined man who would battle hard to bring about the changes he sought. To this end, he told officers at the Department for Education that they were moving towards a potential war footing with schools.

He had read the signs right. Tension in the education system meant that it was heading towards breaking point. Our hero, Brian, and others up and down the nation were about to engage in their own guerrilla war. Brian had grown sick and tired of the constant ill-judged meddling of successive secretaries of state and was already preparing to rebel. He was starting to formulate a highly significant question: would leading the school guided by his own deeply held beliefs – which could mean ignoring his political masters – lead to rack, ruin and destruction, or might it lead his school to somewhere quite exceptional? Some long forgotten Bob Dylan lyrics came drifting into his mind as he realised the time was right to stop being influenced by fools and to start making a different set of rules.[11]

Are You Being Served?

While Rupert Brinton carefully courted popularity with certain influential tabloid newspapers, he certainly didn't get it all his own way with the press. At one stage, some of the more serious papers published articles alluding to the BBC sitcom, *Are You Being Served?* The articles followed revelations from a fellow MP at the Department for Education that Mr Brinton ran the organisation in the same farcical way that 'Young' Mr Grace ran his department store in the classic television sitcom. 'Young' Mr Grace was an octogenarian who usually only said five words at the end of each episode. As he collapsed into the arms of his busty nurse, he told his workforce, 'You've all done very well.' Other articles claimed that bullying was rife in the department and that morale was at rock bottom because civil servants did not believe in the direction being taken.[12]

The Department for Education on a war footing and being run like a sitcom … People were smiling at this stage because it all seemed so trivial. However, the potential for it to descend into chaos that could seriously damage the future life chances of children in the nation's schools was clearly evident. Even at this stage, many might have read these articles and wondered if Rupert Brinton really was a suitable person to be secretary of state for education. The prime minister clearly thought he was.

Chapter 3
The sexy subversive

Smarten up! Scruffy teachers should set an example and dress professionally, says new Ofsted chief

Daily Mail Online, 20 December 2012

Could it possibly work? Could a head teacher truly achieve greatness by ignoring his political masters? Brian knew that more thought was necessary and that every strategic step would need to be planned. He stood up and looked at himself in his full-length mirror. He was a smart man who enjoyed wearing fine clothes. Today he was still wearing the dark Italian designer suit he had worn for work. His white shirt was open at the collar. This had been a deliberate ploy ever since he read a newspaper article saying that Ofsted inspectors ought to inspect the dress code of teachers. This particular article had been written during the Christmas holidays, but as the schools were closed, the reporters had nowhere to visit to take photographs of scruffy teachers with leather arm patches on their jackets, so many based their articles on the BBC television series, *Waterloo Road*. This popular drama tells the fictional tale of a northern comprehensive school. In a typical hour-long episode there could be a kidnapping, a terrorist attack and pupils seducing their teachers, so you can tell it's close to reality.

The fictitious Waterloo Road was located in the Lancashire town of Rochdale. Strangely, on the same day the article appeared, the tabloids failed to report that the town housed only the second sixth form college to be granted outstanding status in England. Aware of the low aspirations in the community, this school had set about daring to be different. They lowered entry requirements and senior leaders drove around the estates to see what made the students tick and what turned them off. They then used this information and developed an approach to teaching that was highly successful. It equipped 83% of students to move on to university. A huge proportion of these young people were the first in their family to do so.[1] However, the *Daily Mail* was not concerned with this major success story and preferred instead to focus on teachers with metaphorical custard stains on their ties.

Brian had stopped wearing a tie because he was determined to find out if a teacher wearing scruffy clothes and a tie would be deemed more suitably dressed than one in smart expensive clothing without a tie. Maybe in a very small way this was an indication of what was to follow. Perhaps he was becoming a radical subversive (if not wearing a tie could be considered subversive). However, in reality he had developed a look which really suited him.

Brian Smith was a tall, dark and athletic man who had maintained his good looks. For five years prior to joining the teaching profession Brian had been a firefighter and over the years he had maintained a good level of fitness. He had left the fire service suddenly. When asked about the reasons why he had changed careers in such a dramatic way, he simply joked that he feared the invention of the domestic smoke alarm would put him out of work. Alternatively, he might quip that Brian Smith was not a suitable name for someone in such a dangerous occupation and it was much more suited to the post of head teacher.

However, Brian's jokes only hid the deep sadness and loss that lay within him. If only he hadn't persuaded Ruth to stay with him for that extra hour she would never have been involved in that horrific road accident. She would have been at home safe and sound, still dreaming of their wedding plans. Instead, a speeding vehicle came round the corner on the wrong side of the road and careered headlong into her car. The extra hour Brian and Ruth had shared that night also proved to be their final hour together. It was Brian's colleagues on Blue Watch who had cut Ruth's lifeless body from the wrecked vehicle.

Prison sentences for those involved did little to ease Brian's sense of devastation. After a while he did pull his life back and build a new career as a teacher, and while he had enjoyed the company of a few attractive women over the years, Brian had remained a bachelor. That devastating experience all those years ago had left Brian scarred and fearful of entering into any kind of relationship that might lead to true love.

There had been moments when it seemed as though this might change. During the previous summer, while holidaying in California, he had met the fabulous Eve who worked in a high-tech post in Silicon Valley. She knew nothing of Brian's past but was intrigued by his present. She studied him with rapt attention when he spoke of the Springett Lane community and England's approaches to educational reform. After Brian had left behind the blue skies and sun of America's west coast for the grey skies and chill of northern England, Eve remained fascinated by a country that seemed intent on developing an education system that looked backwards rather than forwards. Eve really hoped that one day their paths would cross once more because she believed there was unfinished business between them. She used educational issues to remain in email contact with Brian. One such missive ran:

> Hi Bri,
>
> Just been reading in your *Guardian* newspaper that the electronics tycoon James Dyson has been having a bash at Brinton's curriculum plans which seem to downgrade technology to a second rate subject. Now that is dangerous! The UK will end up a second rate country. Leave that old Brinton and his meddlings behind, Brian. Don't let him annoy you. You could get a job out here, and the sun shines all the time too.[2]
>
> Eve x

Maybe it was Eve's emails that were provoking Brian's rise to radicalism!

Doing the right things at the right time in the right way

Eve was not the only person offering Brian guidance. There was also the tall and attractive Andrea. Brian and Andrea regularly met up at a local wine bar. She was a highly effective leadership consultant who had developed her abilities by studying the skills and traits of those very successful people who had deliberately set out to do things differently – the kind of people who had unique ideas and wanted to change the world.

Both Andrea and Brian had recently been watching a rerun of the popular TV series, *Mr Selfridge*, about the shopping magnate, Harry

Gordon Selfridge, as a result of which she had researched his history. Andrea had used this research to develop training programmes for business leaders because she recognised the power of popular culture in education. Selfridge was a man with such an intense energy for the projects he believed in that they called him 'Mile-a-Minute Harry'. He was the man who'd had the idea of trying to make shopping more fun than sex. He revolutionised the appearance of his Oxford Street store to make it a visual as well as tactile experience. He didn't have stock locked away in stuffy oak veneered cabinets; he created enticing central displays in the aisles. He wanted customers to be able to feel the quality of a cashmere shawl or the softness of a pair of kid leather gloves. He lowered wall units and counters and changed the lighting to make the shopping experience more customer friendly. The windows of the store were lit at night so that people could gaze in at the goods on offer. He used publicity better than other department store owners by making sure he cashed in on current affairs, whether they were of human achievement, political elections or even the suffragette movement. He was the master of creating a 'can-do' culture. Where many department stores (especially in London) displayed notices outlining cash fines for staff who might miss a sale, Harry Selfridge posted notices urging his staff:

> To do the right thing at the right time in the right way.
> To do some things better than they have ever been done before.
> To know both sides of the question.
> To be courteous, to be a good example, to anticipate requirements.
> To be satisfied with nothing short of perfection.[3]

These were clearly targets that were qualitative rather than quantitative, with the assumption that if the quality was right, then the quantity of sales would follow. Harry Selfridge was a considerable presence. It was said that just being around him was 'heady stuff'. One person who worked for him was called Homer Buckley and he could recall the impact of working with Selfridge sixty years later: 'he would drop in at your desk, sometimes all of a sudden, sit and talk ten minutes, ask about this and that, never talk down to you – the result was you'd be thrilled for a week. I would literally walk on air after he'd done this at my desk. I never met a man capable of putting such inspiration into his employees.'[4]

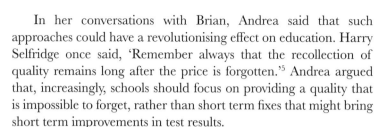
In her conversations with Brian, Andrea said that such approaches could have a revolutionising effect on education. Harry Selfridge once said, 'Remember always that the recollection of quality remains long after the price is forgotten.'[5] Andrea argued that, increasingly, schools should focus on providing a quality that is impossible to forget, rather than short term fixes that might bring short term improvements in test results.

Andrea was developing a powerful bond with Brian. She was ten years younger, but through her considerable knowledge, skills and experience, she was destined to fan the flames of the Springett Lane revolution. Andrea was significant in shaping Brian's thinking, but he was unaware that there was an underlying reason for her interest in Springett Lane. She was being driven and energised by her own intense moral purpose.

Life changing butterflies

So there were Eve's emails and there was advice from Andrea, but there was also a third figure guiding Brian towards an educational revolution. The brilliant Tom Featherstone had been the local authority adviser to the selection panel at the time of Brian's controversial appointment to the headship of Springett Lane. In Tom's time he too had been an inspirational head teacher, but he had moved on to lead the school improvement service where he had become responsible for all the town's primary schools.

To everyone's surprise, Tom had recently retired. He said that one day, totally out of the blue, he realised that it was time to call it a day. As a consequence of the Springett Lane interviews, Councillor Roger Stonehouse sought revenge on Tom for defying his wishes and started bombarding him with requests for ridiculous bits of information and data. He wanted Tom out of the local authority and used any method he could to achieve his aim. Rapidly, the tension grew between them until one evening at a social event, Councillor Stonehouse strode towards Tom and announced, 'I would like to talk to you about the low English standards achieved in this town by the children who are new arrivals to the country.' Tom knew that this was neither the time nor the place for this type of conversation, and without a second thought he simply responded, 'And I would like you to clear off and leave me alone.' Unsurprisingly, that represented the precise moment Tom realised that it was time to call it a day.

He had also become tired of political interference. Secretaries of state were constantly telling teachers how to do their jobs. He had pondered on whether Rupert Brinton would tell brain surgeons how to operate if he was ever moved to the Department for Health. He suspected he would.

Brian already had huge respect for Tom who had acted as a school improvement partner to Springett Lane in the past, and he continued to seek his advice even after his departure from the local authority. During his illustrious career, Tom had become a great advocate of the work of Sir Tim Brighouse. Part of this was due to the fact he once sued a previous education secretary for calling him a 'madman' during a speech at the 1993 Tory party conference.[6] Tom had very little time for political interference by novices in the education system. He also really admired the 'butterflies' approach promoted by Sir Brighouse, who believed that often it is the little things a leader does that have the greatest impact. He called this approach the 'butterfly effect'.[7] It is based on the notion that, under certain conditions, the whirring of a butterfly's wings in the Amazonian rainforest can affect the climate elsewhere, even to the extent of creating a tornado in North America. Tom recognised that if such little things can bring chaos, then little things can also lead to brilliance and, if a leader focuses on small things, it can have a disproportionate effect on the success of an organisation.

Tom's collection of butterflies was about to help transform Brian's thinking and Springett Lane Primary School forever. However, Tom's support brought other insights which would allow Brian to fight his guerrilla war. Tom knew about how central government, sometimes with the support of Ofsted, would use bullying and threatening tactics in order to achieve some of their less popular policies or vanity projects. As a result of Tom's insider knowledge, Brian knew that Springett Lane could easily make it onto the Department for Education's list of schools whose autonomy they would like to see removed. The education system was heading to a point where all the power in education lay in the hands of one person – the secretary of state.

Brian checks out the research

Brian continued to stare into the mirror. His puzzled expression reflected back at him. Then he said out loud: 'Rupert Brinton may say he is a traditionalist when it comes to education but I am not so sure. I don't know what he is but he isn't a traditionalist!' His anger was rising. 'Forget it,' he said to himself. 'Brinton is just like all the other politicians pontificating all over the place to make himself sound good.' He had a deep mistrust of politicians, as did the rest of the nation who regarded them as less trustworthy than the bankers who had brought the economy to its knees in 2008.

Members of parliament from all political parties seem to have an intense love of league tables. However, they seemed to take very little notice of their ranking in the aforementioned Ipsos MORI poll of people trusted to tell the truth. The two least trusted professions were politicians in general and government ministers specifically. Even worse was the fact that too many politicians found themselves embroiled in fraudulent expenses claims such as buying duck houses for their country estates with taxpayers' money or taking bungs to lobby parliament. *Private Eye* reported that a member of parliament in Britain is four times more likely to go to prison than other members of society.[8]

The problem was that Brian couldn't forget it. He certainly knew that the secretary of state was not a traditionalist and set about trying to prove it. He scanned the bookshelves in his apartment. He was not looking for the glossy paperbacks of the modern era, but for the hardbacks with cloth covers; the kind of book you gently stroked as you considered the wisdom within. It was as though the sensory experience enriched the understanding. The first book he pulled off the shelf was a red hardback entitled *Primary Education* produced by the Department of Education and Science in 1959.[9] This was a time when the inspectorate was deemed to be an organisation that was independent of politicians rather than their puppets. Brian remembered buying the book at a second-hand bookshop several years ago, and he now thought to himself that it was bound to be a traditional text as even the pages had turned from white to a yellowy cream. The name of the first owner, Patricia Martin, had been beautifully handwritten using a fountain pen in a 'Marion Richardson' style on the inside cover.

At the time of its publication, Harold Macmillan had led the Conservatives to a third successive term in office, declaring that 'we must try to emphasise the fundamental unity of our people and not exaggerate the differences that divide us'.[10] This ideal had certainly not been achieved at Springett Lane half a century later. The book was from a time when those who were fortunate enough to own a black and white television settled down and watched the traditional policing by *Dixon of Dock Green* and listened to the music of Frank Sinatra and Connie Francis on the gramophone. If you did endorse the traditional values of working hard, and for long enough, you might be able to buy a brand new Austin 7 motor car for £500. This was the era when summers were proper traditional summers with blue skies and sunshine, and the temperature rose above 70°F (21°C) for a third of the year in some parts of Britain. The beaches were full and you could buy pots of tea to drink on the sand. How much more traditional could it get?

The book fell open to give him a snapshot of what life was really like in our schools during this period. Brian found no mention of children sitting in rows reciting poetry or knowing the kings and queens of England. It seemed to speak, not about children receiving instruction seated at the isolation of their desk, but of them learning in a social context where they took responsibility for making their own choices in education:

> The primary school curriculum … has gradually been enriched and liberalised as more generous and enlightened views have prevailed and as conditions have made a fuller and better education of children possible. Public opinion has now accepted the principle that education should be concerned with the all-round development of each child according to his age and capacity and that this education should aim at making him a better member of the community, spiritually, morally, physically and intellectually. The traditional curriculum is therefore very differently interpreted from the way in which it was originally conceived.[11]

Brian flicked through the pages once more until he found one with several words underlined. He started to read once more:

> The task of education is two-fold. It has to enable children to grow up as good members of the societies in which they live and this entails their developing to a sufficient degree of

conformity to the ways of those societies. At the same time, it is expected to develop in them a proper sense of independence in thought and action, which implies a power to choose and to make judgements on their own account.[12]

Brian read the words several times and by now he was convinced that the learning opportunities being promoted felt very different from those experienced by the children now sitting in rows and potentially learning by rote. It seemed to stress that the best learning did not occur with the teacher standing at the front of the class as the font of all knowledge and transmitting it to the thirty children in front of him or her. Brian knew that many of the adults who had experienced this kind of approach associated it with boredom and fear. He thought of the words Einstein had used to describe his own education: 'One had to cram all this stuff into one's mind for the examinations, whether one liked it or not. This coercion had such a deterring effect on me ...'[13]

'Well, clearly either I have got things wrong or Rupert Brinton has,' Brian thought to himself. 'Or maybe I have simply selected the wrong decade.' He skimmed along his shelves once more until he pulled out a rather grey and delicate book written in the 1930s, a time when the FA Cup was won by the so-called unfashionable football clubs with long names that they didn't share with anybody else, such as Preston North End, Sheffield Wednesday and West Bromwich Albion. Britain lived in a make-do-and-mend culture as it approached the Second World War.

This book had been written by the Board of Education, which was the Ofsted of a bygone age. There was a series of adverts at the start of the volume, one of which said that the era of the blackboard had come to an end following the advent of the 'Ellams Duplicator'. The book even advised female teachers what kind of corsets they should wear to be comfortable in the classroom. As Brian read, he started to find himself not so much in educational commentary but knee deep in sex-role stereotyping and dirty washing:

The Science of Laundry work: In dealing with the theoretical side of laundry work, close cooperation between the courses in needlework and science will develop a critical attitude to the composition of materials used in ready-made clothing and their reaction to washing processes. The various ingredients used in laundry work should be studied experimentally and their physical reactions observed. Hardness of water supplied, quality of soap, value of washing powder and similar commercial products, costs of materials for washday are only some of the issues, which may be profitably discussed.

Cost and quality of materials should be carefully considered in a practical way. The amount and cost of soap used for each class for example may be recorded and the teacher and the girls will learn to secure economy by careful checking of stores and price.

Changing conditions in housing, particularly the increase of flat dwellings, the limitation of drying facilities and the difficulties involved in open air drying are all important aspects of laundry work and subjects for consideration in laundry lessons.[14]

The text conjured up a picture in Brian's mind of a different age, when men and women had more traditional roles to fulfil, and he concluded that this must be Rupert Brinton's golden period. Brian then realised that it seemed to be based on a more forward thinking pedagogy which was about cross-curricular approaches, experimentation, financial literacy, enterprise and relevant practical activities. Not only that, the same message was reiterated time and again throughout the text, with no mention of children learning best by being seated in rows and reciting poetry.

Brian thought carefully and concluded that all the research he had read suggested that the secretary of state was wrong. He had always been aware that the general public tended to spend more time believing failed teachers, politicians and tabloid reporters than successful school leaders. This was despite the fact that the Audit Commission had regularly found that the local primary school was among the most respected organisations within a local community.[15]

Furthermore, Brian's thinking had proved to him that the secretary of state was a dangerous meddler and it was time for him to make a stand – the one that would turn him into a truly inspirational and outstanding school leader. Decisive action was required so he prepared to rebel against government policy.

He imagined Winston Churchill standing there with his right hand tucked into his jacket, pulling on a huge cigar and uttering the words, 'Head teachers have an autonomy that politicians can only dream of.' Well, Brian was determined to use this autonomy, but knew he would need a very clear leadership plan for the future. He leaned across his laptop, which was lying idle, and picked up his notepad and pen. In selecting pen and paper over the laptop he hoped he had not become a traditionalist. In Churchillian style he said out loud as he wrote:

> My sole purpose is to create a learning community where every child and adult achieves, has a duty to achieve and has a duty to help others achieve.

Is the 'hokey cokey' really what it's all about?

Meanwhile, there was more bad news for Rupert Brinton in the quality newspapers. A series of articles had claimed that young people were being deprived of a rounded education, as his proposed examination reforms were treating the arts like the 'hokey cokey'. One minute they were in and the next they were out. The accusations against Mr Brinton suggested that thousands of young people were being denied the chance to study art, music and computer science.[16] The secretary of state's response was to assert that his critics were linked to a network of Marxist academics in teacher training colleges and universities. On one occasion it was suggested that the arts should be accessed by young people through Saturday morning classes and clubs. In the award-winning film, *Billy Elliot*, would Mr Elliot have got out of bed to take his son to Saturday morning ballet classes? The most likely answer is no. As a consequence, others accused Rupert Brinton of making the arts accessible only to the middle and upper classes.

People were still smiling but some had started to feel uneasy …

Chapter 4

Every time I use my mobile phone I take a photograph of my foot

Teachers wear body armour to stop unruly pupils biting them

Daily Mail Online, 16 April 2009

1. Who was married to Eleanor of Aquitaine?
2. The figure 1 followed by 100 zeros is known as what?
3. Which monarch was known as the wisest fool in Christendom?
4. Which county cricket side is based at Chester-le-Street?
5. What was the occupation of the composer Borodin?
6. If you planted the seeds of *Quercus robur* what would grow?
7. Why am I asking these questions?

They were just seven questions that Brian had drafted, but they changed the way the staff at Springett Lane Primary School thought about their school curriculum. If you knew the answers to any of the first six questions it could have made you a very rich person. They have been million pound questions in the popular television quiz show *Who Wants To Be a Millionaire?* Brian had taken them into the weekly professional development meeting to prove a point, and it worked brilliantly. One of the teachers called Ray was a keen sports fan and instantly knew that Durham played cricket matches at Chester-le-Street (worryingly, he could also list all other first class cricket venues used in England over the last century, including the one at Hastings which is now a supermarket), but the rest of the staff drew a blank on all the other questions.

Brian had then asked the staff to get out any smartphones to see how long it would take them to find the answers to the remaining five questions. The answers were found within fifty-five seconds, an average of nine seconds per question, reflecting the availability and speed of information in the twenty-first century.

However, the seventh question remains unanswered – well, at least for the time being. Why had Brian asked the questions in the first place (because he very nearly hadn't)? In fact, this professional development meeting proved to be a very significant turning point in the history of Springett Lane. You probably want to know why it was so significant. To understand that, the story needs to rewind forty-eight hours.

Imagination is more important than knowledge[1]

It was Sunday morning and Brian sat with a cup of coffee, brooding over yet another misleading story from the *Daily Mail*. He may have been on his own but he read the headline out loud: 'Teachers wear body armour to stop unruly pupils biting them'. This seemed the most ludicrous headline to date. He imagined head teachers leading the early morning briefing sessions in the staffroom where, instead of teachers gulping down the final dregs of instant coffee, they were busy strapping on their bulletproof vests ready for another gruelling day taking bakery classes and teaching phonics with Year 1. The thought was ridiculous. In his years as a teacher, deputy head and head, he had never encountered a teacher who had been bitten by a pupil, and even if this did occasionally happen elsewhere, these cannibalistic children would not go for the torso but the more accessible extremities like the arms, hands or fingers. However, on reflection Brian did concede that, if the children's education was really dull and unimaginative, they might just bite the nearest person out of a deep sense of frustration. Indeed, he thought of Anne Moody's class where every morning blank-faced, yawning children dutifully started their day silently doing their routine non-negotiable decontextualised tasks relating to word and sentence level work.

Brian moved on through the newspaper and found the latest pronouncements from the secretary of state, this time asserting that children needed to learn more facts in school. Rupert Brinton had announced that there had been too much emphasis on the methods of teaching rather than the learning of facts.[2] As usual, the minister was wrong. Without consideration being given to teaching style or methods, any facts taught would most likely be instantly forgotten. Besides, Brian knew that so many facts were simply available at the touch of a button, so schools needed to be built around something different.

Undeterred, Brian started to trawl the internet to see what else the dreaded Brinton had been saying recently about the curriculum, and identified a number of concerns the secretary of state had about the teaching of British history and how schools should be focusing more on the glories of our past rather than issues such as the Holocaust.[3] It is certainly true that Britain has been a great political and economic power, but maybe some of that power derived from less glorious historic events. For three centuries, great wealth was created through the slave trade. During the Industrial Revolution, the wealthy 10% regularly exploited the poorer 90% by exposing them to gruelling and dangerous working conditions. In the First World War, over 300 volunteer soldiers were shot at dawn for alleged desertion. Those responsible claimed it was good for the morale of the men to see 'examples' being made. It is now accepted that many of those executed were suffering from shell shock or what we now refer to as post-traumatic stress disorder.

Brian started to trawl once more. He was now looking for something very specific in order to find a more contrasting view of history teaching, and found it when he discovered a list of the top quotations relating to history. Instinctively he found himself trying to knit them together. He started to write:

> What we really know about history:
>   While history can be a vast early warning system, too often it never says goodbye; it only says 'See you later' as it has a tendency to repeat itself, often as tragedy. In periods where there is no leadership society stands still. Real progress only occurs when skilful, empathetic and imaginative leaders strive to change things for the better. Their courage becomes contagious and hope takes on a life of its own.

In the end, thought Brian, history is all about imagination rather than facts.

The secretary of state seemed to be taking the Thomas Gradgrind approach of 'Teach[ing] these boys and girls nothing but Facts.'[4] Suddenly Brian's thinking had sharpened because, once again, he realised that the Right Honourable Rupert Brinton was taking too simplistic a view. The facts were only a part of successful history teaching. The children had to be encouraged to *feel* what it was like to be born into a slave family, or to work in arduous conditions in an eighteenth century factory, or to be entrenched in a First World War battlefield waiting to charge into no man's land. It was those courageous leaders who developed this kind of empathy who genuinely changed the world for the better.

Brian wrote:

> The importance of feelings in education:
> What if we were to plan for how children feel at the end of a lesson, especially if it leaves them with a heightened sense of empathy or anger about injustice, or with a desire to change the world for the better?

Brian continued to think, and half an idea came to mind (which was destined to return at a later stage). He had realised that what was needed was not simply facts but imagination. It was about being able to use the facts in order to imagine what a better world might look like. The long forgotten words of Einstein came back to him. He reached for his pen and notebook and wrote down: 'Imagination is more important than knowledge.'

Just then a new email pinged in from Eve in California:

> Hi Bri,
> Just been scouring the internet and read that your nearest and dearest rivals, the French, are revising their national curriculum, with the emphasis being placed on children learning how to live good lives, distinguishing vice from virtue and justice from injustice. They argue that this is what the current generation needs to live fulfilled lives and to solve some of the major problems in the world.

Seems a little different and more forward looking than
anything from Brinton. Shall we move to the sunny south
of France, Bri?[5]

Eve x

Brian suddenly found himself thinking about a concerned parent
he had been speaking to recently. Each week he worked six shifts
at a local distribution warehouse. Each shift had been scientifically
designed to be divided into four sessions, with two fifteen minute
breaks and a forty minute lunch break. He had to achieve a target
of completing seventy packages per session. That's a total of 280
packages a day and 1,680 per week. He rarely remembered any
of the packages. His day-to-day life was unremarkable and unin-
teresting. Indeed, he spent much of his time at work daydreaming.

His son, Brett, went to the local primary school five days a week.
Each day was divided into four sessions with two fifteen minute
breaks and a forty-five minute lunch break. Each lesson was broken
down into three parts. There was an overriding learning objective
and three differentiated learning intentions. Over the course of a
week, Brett experienced twenty learning objectives, which he rarely
remembered, and sixty learning intentions, forty of which did not
apply to him. His day-to-day life was unremarkable and uninter-
esting, and he spent much of his time daydreaming.

Brian suddenly became concerned that there was a danger that
his school was becoming a distribution warehouse for teaching and
not a centre for the creation of learning.

Brett's lack of attention had triggered the meeting with his
father. His teachers were also growing increasingly concerned
about his lack of concentration. Brian had started to worry about
how many other children seemed to drift off in lessons. Were
these children daydreaming, and, if so, what were they daydreaming about? Brian could remember reading an article by Paul
McCartney who claimed that he passed through his secondary
education daydreaming about music and what a better world
might look like.[6]

Maybe children daydreaming in school is on the increase. Brian
had recently watched a short film by Sir Ken Robinson entitled
'Changing Education Paradigms' in which he argues that children

are being overwhelmed by technology in the form of computers, smartphones and tablets and, consequently, being penalised for switching off at school because they find it boring.[7] In the film, Robinson questions whether the rise in diagnoses for attention deficit hyperactivity disorder (ADHD) reflects dull lessons and the growth of standardised testing. Brian reflected and reached for his notepad to write:

What do children dream about, and how do we tap into these dreams?

He was fairly convinced that these were the last questions a politician would ask – and the last thing they would be interested in – and therefore this had to be the right direction in which to proceed.

Brian reached for his mobile phone. He wanted to arrange to meet up with Andrea, but the darned thing had gone missing again. He knew he spent far more time looking for his phone than using it. 'How come I can never find that phone?!' he uttered out loud in frustration. The answer was quite obvious: it's far easier to find big things, but with the numerous different generations of mobiles, they had become smaller and thinner. That thought set Brian off once more. He counted to four on his fingers and thought, 'If we are on the fourth generation of mobile phones, what generation of the curriculum are we on, and why doesn't it move at the same pace as the rest of life? Perhaps the curriculum should become smaller and thinner?'

Technology did not interest Brian, nor was he very good at using it. For Brian, sending a text message could be as fast as using second-class post. He was frequently in the bizarre situation of taking a photograph of his foot every time the phone rang. He was vaguely aware that the improvements made during the different generations of phones related to the move from analogue to digital, the speed of connectivity and the use of broadband and Wi-Fi. However, what Brian did understand was that, over time, mobile phones had increasingly provided the technology required to live a full life in the twenty-first century. The appropriate tapping of a screen would organise his diary for the day, allow him to send and receive emails and access the internet, tell him how his favourite football team was performing, take photographs and, should he ever need to, he could even make a phone call.

Brian knew that the first generation of mobile phones had arrived in the late 1980s, coincidentally around the time of the introduction of the national curriculum in English schools. It arrived as part of the legislation within the Education Reform Act. Brian had clarity about the things that a mobile phone could do today that it couldn't in 1988, but he wasn't immediately sure how the national curriculum had progressed over the same period. Many experts considered that these years had been a bleak time, dominated by heavy prescription, testing, targets and league tables, all of which had led to an impoverished curriculum. Professor Robin Alexander had once suggested that over time the curriculum had hardly moved at all:

> English primary education in 2000 is the nineteenth century elementary education modified – much modified admittedly – rather than transformed. Elementary education is at its centre of gravity. Elementary education provides its central point of reference. Elementary education is the form to which it most readily tends to regress.[8]

However, Brian found himself taking an alternative view. Over these years there had been a huge financial investment in education. Tony Blair had been elected prime minister in 1997 claiming that his three priorities for government were 'education, education, education'. Some of the changes had been positive but others less so. Brian reached for his pen and notebook and started to draw up a table. He found that in the quarter of a century since the advent of the national curriculum, in most schools there had been at least three different generations of the curriculum. He recorded his thoughts systematically:

The first-generation curriculum	Key features
1988 onwards The 'moving to conformity' period	Key focus on the 3Rs. Pupil progress was monitored through national curriculum Attainment Levels. The focus was predominantly on the coverage of national programmes of study. As a consequence, children experienced prescribed but often tame themes, such as 'Invaders and Settlers', 'Earth and Space' and 'Night and Day' as well as other words linked by 'and'.

A beacon dims

Many people had commented that she was Moody by name and moody by nature, but that had not always been the case. Her maiden name had been Anne Knight and she had joined the teaching staff at Springett Lane Primary School in 1980. She remembered very well the era about which Brian had scribbled his notes. At that stage she had been an extremely attractive young teacher and her first head teacher had been very shocked at the length of her skirts. One day he had decided that something needed to be said in order to protect decency in the school. However, he didn't do this until he had been into her classroom at least five times to have a good stare and check on just how shocked he was. The next day she had come in wearing a longer skirt, for which the head teacher grudgingly thanked her before suggesting that maybe a little less cleavage should be on show the following day. It almost broke his heart, but finally he insisted that she look at herself in the mirror and if she could see up it, down it or through it, she should change it!

It was not all bad news for Anne Knight during this period. At this stage she had been a Knight by name and by nature, and she fought for all the things she valued in education. She had quickly been promoted, and rightly so. In those days her teaching practice shone out like a beacon as she weaved a web of magic with her children. She enjoyed the freedom of the age and her creativity knew no bounds. Her initial teacher training had awakened in her the joy that teaching can bring. The principal of the college once commented to her, 'I remember visiting a school in London's Docklands and the lights were on because a ship was blocking out the sun as the children used their textbooks to study Southampton Docks.'[9] There was a period of silence while Anne Knight considered the wisdom of these words. She then realised that the quality of the focused active learning experience was all-important and tried to encapsulate that spirit. The children read and wrote, drew and danced with stunning skill, pride and sensitivity as they explored their environment and locality through their first hand experiences in all four seasons. The starting point of many projects was the locality because it could be used at any time, in any season and as often as you needed. From that point children would move out to investigate wider issues. As a consequence, they understood their community and developed a deep sense of identity within their nation so they knew its place within their world.

For Anne Knight, the arrival of the national curriculum was like being fitted with a straitjacket. She hated the prescriptiveness of the programmes of study, which she found tame, abstract and bland. There no longer seemed to be the time to create an ethic of excellence and achieve outcomes of genuine quality. The emphasis was now on covering things rather than deep learning. The waves of electricity that used to pulse through her as she saw the children communicate, reflect and express their learning with stunning quality were lost. One night, in desperation, she reflected upon these many lost opportunities. She picked up her pen and started to write:

> As I look around me I seem to see everything that is wrong with the world. I see tensions between nations and within nations. People seem to care so little for the planet and they have no concern for the generations that will live on it in the future. And yet if you look closely beauty is all around us. The trouble is most of us rarely see it. We simply race past in some form of perpetual hurry. Every second we're alive represents a new and unique moment in the history of the universe. It's

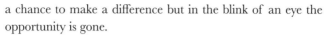

a chance to make a difference but in the blink of an eye the opportunity is gone.

If I ask myself what my contribution has been, the answer would be that it's minimal. I have been too busy pointing to the lines of latitude and longitude on a projected image in a classroom rather than taking children to the source of a river where water bubbles magically from the ground. They have been given worksheets about Neolithic hunter-gatherers and yet have never opened their eyes to the rich diversity of people who make up their local community in the twenty-first century. I have stood by while visits to the locality and engagement with the arts have been replaced by specially designed national curriculum programmes or textbooks produced by Messrs Nelson, Ginn and Macmillan because the education system believes they guarantee full coverage of the prescribed knowledge children need to have.

The opportunities were indeed lost and each weekend Anne Knight dutifully ticked the boxes recording what each child had covered, and allegedly learned, in their individual record books. The ticks in the boxes stated that the children had been taught that Henry VIII had six wives, that the Cairngorms were a mountain range in Scotland and that there was a special force called gravity that pulled things towards the earth. While Anne Knight remained conscientious and did as she was asked, sadly she was no longer a weaver of magic for the children.

The second-generation curriculum: conform or else

Brian switched on his desk lamp and considered the second generation of the curriculum, recording the following thoughts in his notebook. He considered that they reflected a bleak time in curriculum design for schools.

The second-generation curriculum	Key features
1998 onwards The 'ball and chain' years	Increased prescription through the advent of the literacy strategy, numeracy strategy and QCA schemes of work meant there was a move towards a subject based curriculum. An increased emphasis on testing and pupils' progress via sub-levels and average points. Teachers moved towards transmitting information that they believed would help the children to pass tests. There was a shift towards teaching exam techniques and providing booster lessons. Ofsted inspect the delivery of each subject area, complete with work scrutiny on four-day inspections.

It is easier to count the bottles than judge the quality of the wine[11]

Anne Knight, now Moody, also remembered the period from 1998 onward well. By that point she had two children and it was a time that had included a very acrimonious divorce. Life was very stressful and support from school leaders had been minimal. Maybe under different circumstances things would have been different. The truth was that everybody was under pressure. Achieving high standards in the form of test results in a school like Springett Lane would always be a huge year-on-year challenge. The school battened down the hatches because they were fearful of having poor results followed by an unfavourable Ofsted inspection. Half-termly assessments in the form of tests and the use of optional SATs for each year group led to children constantly being prepared for examinations. After this, there would be the inevitable questions asked of teachers if it was not possible for them to demonstrate pupil progress. Too often this was replicated all over England's schools, with the nation's young people becoming the most tested in the world. Some teachers spoke of their level 3b children rather than using their names. Research showed that during the schooldays of a typical young person, they spent a full year either preparing for tests, being tested or recovering from tests.[12] Our children get just one childhood and this seems an appalling way to spend it.

During the period of her divorce, Anne Moody was deeply unhappy both at home and at school. She never cried in front of the children, but she did cry on her way to school, on her way home from school and each night as she sought the sanctuary of sleep. Members of the leadership team should always notice what is going on in people's lives, but in her case they didn't. Most good leaders know that helping staff when they need it is like putting money in the bank, because it is always paid back with interest. The leaders took no interest in Anne Moody and, consequently, no interest was received in return.

The arrival of national frameworks and schemes of work did remove some of the pressure. These documents told teachers what to do and when to do it. The capacity to keep recycling the same lessons year on year removed a burden around planning. However, it also removed any element of spontaneity and stifled career development, with many teachers not seeking promotion in other schools because they knew what they were doing in their current setting. Anne had been in numerous staff meetings on the introduction of the various nationally prescribed curriculum packages, and on each occasion she asked, 'Are these materials compulsory?' and received the reply, 'No, but they are a national expectation and Ofsted will find it very difficult to inspect us if we aren't using them.' By asking these questions, Anne became perceived as a blocker of progress and was increasingly marginalised by the school's leaders.

It has to be said that the materials had incorporated many good ideas designed to engage primary aged pupils, but for the majority of schools the 'one size fits all' curriculum had arrived. Many Ofsted inspectors breathed a sigh of relief when they knew that each child had a separate exercise book for each subject and that each subject was being taught through the nationally prescribed frameworks.

Anne Moody spent these years in her classroom designing slippers and pizza toppings and covering mundane word and sentence level work that did very little to emphasise the beauty of the English language. Her passion and creativity were being quashed. Sadly, this story was repeated for many other teachers in many other schools.

Some make things happen, some watch things happen and some wonder what happened

A huge smile spread across Brian's face as he thought about the third-generation curriculum. He was a deputy head at his previous school during the 2000s when the doors were opening to more exciting times. The more forward thinking school leaders were moving away from the national guidance and examining research into how people really learn and the traits of successful learners. New and exciting thinking that was more in line with the twenty-first century seemed to be coming from the government. A previous (and more enlightened) secretary of state for education had stated that, as a government, they stood accused of taking the enjoyment and pleasure, which should be the birth right of every child, out of education.[13] The period started with *Excellence and Enjoyment*, which urged all schools to take full responsibility for the curriculum,[14] and culminated in the Rose Review of the national curriculum, which proposed increased flexibility and a curriculum based around newly defined essentials for learning and life.[15]

The smile had appeared on Brian's face because his school had embraced the freedom of that period. However, other schools had not, and even Her Majesty's Chief Inspector of Schools acknowledged that the reason for this was a debilitating sense of fear. The pressure to keep raising standards remained intense.[16] Each new Ofsted framework led to an increase in the number of schools deemed to be failing. While Brian's then school had moved forward with an exciting skills based curriculum, Springett Lane during this period had remained fearful of any drop in results and that led to a mundane curriculum with a focus on the core subjects being taught in a highly prescriptive way. Most schools rigidly introduced three-part lessons as promoted by the National Strategies, and school inspectors prowled around checking that there was regular use of learning intentions, open-ended questions, talk partners, differentiation by task and plenaries. Sadly, as a result, the third-generation

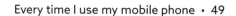

curriculum did not arrive everywhere. A famous quote came to mind and Brian quickly scribbled it down in his notepad:

> There are three kinds of people: those who make things happen, those who watch things happen and those who ask what happened.[17]

Brian continued to record his thoughts:

The third-generation curriculum	Key features
Some made things happen, some watched what happened and others asked what happened	Increased attention placed on the science of pedagogy through the use of developing three-part lessons, a focus on learning intentions, differentiating learning tasks by ability groups, and the use of plenaries and mini-plenaries. Shift towards the children as learners through such things as: • The social and emotional aspects of learning.[18] • Learning styles.[19] • Guy Claxton's Building Learning Power.[20] • Howard Gardner's intelligences.[21] • Arthur Costa's Habits of Mind.[22] • Schools start to select their own drivers such as thinking skills or enterprise education, as suggested by the Cambridge Primary Review.[23] • Some schools adopt the principles of Sir Jim Rose's review of the national curriculum.[24]

The third-generation curriculum never arrived at Springett Lane Primary School, and it certainly didn't arrive in the classroom of Anne Moody. There was a good reason for this. As initiative followed initiative her confidence descended through a downwards spiral. It felt as though every adverse newspaper headline was aimed at her. As a consequence she stopped questioning the system and started to question herself. Indeed, she wondered if her methods had ever been appropriate and whether or not she, and those like her, had been responsible for providing children with an inappropriate education. With her self-esteem at rock bottom and the former sparkle in her eyes lost, Anne Moody's classroom became a safe and sterile environment. Sadly, the school's leaders left her alone and she tended to leave them alone. This was a tragedy as they had so much to offer each other.

If I was educated I would be a damn fool[25]

Brian knew he had to plan the professional development meeting that would take him further forward. He had wanted to call it a staff meeting, but he had been told that this term belonged to a different and long past era. That was when he had hit upon the idea of the six questions from the quiz show *Who Wants To Be a Millionaire?* as outlined in the opening of this chapter. He knew that this simple exercise could demonstrate that information is available at the touch of a button but that inspiration isn't. The seventh question was, 'Why am I asking these questions?' The reggae singer Bob Marley was born into poverty in Jamaica, but when he arrived at school, he announced he didn't want to be given information but was looking for inspiration and aspiration. Brian wanted the same for Springett Lane.

Brian did locate his mobile phone, only to find a text from Andrea that she had sent almost two hours earlier. The message simply said, 'Been thinking a lot about u and your project. Fancy the wine bar tonight … 8.00?' Brian hurriedly but belatedly accepted the invitation, and quickly got the response, 'C U L8r. XXX'.

Meanwhile, there was further bad press for Rupert Brinton as the media reported on a crisis of confidence at the Department for Education where six out of ten employees did not consider it safe to challenge the way things were now being done and only one in four considered that the changes were for the better. Staff claimed that they were working permanently in a climate of fear. The National Audit Office accused the secretary of state for education of running a 'dysfunctional department'.[26]

Chapter 5
Wanted: invisible leaders – apply here

Schools to get surprise Ofsted inspections ... to catch out naughty teachers

Daily Mail Online, 15 July 2011

Andrea was scheduled to meet Brian at 8 p.m., but as the digital clock flicked over to 7.30, she knew she was going to be late. She was excited by the potential of Brian's project but on a personal level she was also deeply worried.

Like Brian, Andrea's father had been the head teacher of a school in an area of significant disadvantage. She had watched him over the years and known that he was a warm-hearted man and a truly exceptional leader. Andrea had always accepted that working in challenging communities was not for the faint-hearted. Not only did such schools have to operate in an area of poverty and challenge, but they also had to compete against the inspectorate and various government agencies, which frequently lowered morale by imposing every insulting and derogatory title they could upon the school, describing them as having serious weaknesses, coasting or even being 'hard to shift' (a term introduced by the National Strategies). Andrea's father worked extremely hard and with sheer determination had led his school through all of these insulting labels and created an exceptional learning community. She glanced down at a range of personal memorabilia that she always kept with her. It was spread across the dressing table.

There was the newspaper headline which announced: 'A community weeps for the loss of brilliant head teacher'. The local MP had described feeling devastated to hear of her father's untimely death. She had described him as exceptional and inspirational, and stated that she had witnessed his hard work, dedication and care for his pupils. His exceptional talents had been reflected in the school's most recent excellent Ofsted report.

Andrea now turned her attention to that inspection report. It had been written just two weeks before his death. She started to read: 'This is a good school that has outstanding features. The children get off to a flying start and make good progress throughout the rest of their schooling. The excellent leadership of the head teacher enables the school to play an active role in the community and provide high quality care and guidance for pupils and their families. The school does not stand still. The head teacher provides decisive leadership which motivates and empowers staff, pupils, parents and carers and this drives ambition and embeds a culture of improvement.' She hadn't needed to read the words. They were imprinted on her mind and ingrained in her heart. It was the last sentence in particular that had intrigued her. She believed that her father had developed a particular talent that she called 'invisible leadership', and this was a concept she had explored, hoping that her work might allow his legacy to live on.

At this stage Andrea did not want Brian to know anything about this part of her life. She wanted to look professional at all times, and she was fearful that any discussions about her family history may result in her not being able to control her emotions. She had also pledged to her mother never to become romantically involved with a school leader as the toll on their family had been too great.

Brian was sitting at a table alone when Andrea pushed open the glass doors of the wine bar at 8.10. She was looking fabulous and the conversation quickly started to flow. Then Andrea looked at Brian and said, 'I have been thinking about you a lot, and especially about your project.' In response, Brian started to explain how he wanted to create a fourth-generation curriculum for Springett Lane, at a time when it hadn't even embraced a third-generation curriculum.

Andrea added, 'Well, I think I can help because after our last meeting I decided to check out some information, and much of what happens in schools is replicated in businesses all over the country.' Then she asked, 'Do you still have your notebook because you need to remember this.' Brian handed over the pad and pen and Andrea started to write:[1]

> The problems with UK schools and organisations:
>
> * Most UK organisations are over-managed and under-led.
> * Strong leadership with weak management is no better.
> * The real challenge is to combine strong leadership and strong management.
> * Leader-managers are what both schools and organisations need.
> * Institutionalising a leader/manager-centred culture is the ultimate act of leadership.

Andrea put down the pen and started to speak once more: 'There is one thing schools are crying out for, and that is leaders with vision. As part of my research I've been speaking with lots of teachers, and do you know that, within about five minutes, I can get them to start talking about their head teachers? Every school day of every school year, far harsher critics than Ofsted sit in your staffroom, and one of the things that dominates their conversation is the quality of leadership and management. Every time I have such a conversation, it falls into one of three scenarios. In the worst case, the teachers simply complain about the things the head doesn't do, whether it's taking assemblies or regularly visiting classrooms. Some even complained that they didn't always attend the weekly professional development meetings. Thankfully, not too many described that kind of head teacher.

'Most spoke about the positive things that the head actually did, such as leading extra-curricular events, learning walks around the school, pupil interviews or even sending members of staff home when they were unwell, then promptly rolling up their sleeves and teaching their class. However, only rarely did I hit the absolute jackpot and get an account of what the head teacher passionately believed in, and that is what 80% of the teachers I spoke to were desperate to hear.

'I understand the problems, Brian. The accountability is intense and the price of failure huge. The bold and the strong are needed

more than ever. I think there are basically four types of school leader out there, with several hybrids in-between.' She reached for the pen and notebook once more. This time she started to draw as well as write: [2]

THE INVISIBLE MANAGER

The key organisational structures are there. There is a degree of predictability and order. Planning and pupil progress data is collected (although little is done with it). Budgets are set and stuck to. The staff know this person is there somewhere and the school runs smoothly but teachers regularly complain about a lack of presence. He/she is difficult to track down and often works behind closed doors or is regularly out of school.

THE VISIBLE MANAGER

Is also fully focused on the key organisational structures and the school runs smoothly. However, this person is highly visible around the school, and may well be involved in classrooms and lead or be involved in a club or society as well as teaching some lessons. He/she is approachable and regularly seeks out the staff. He/she is supportive and encouraging and the staff like him/her for this. However, the emphasis remains on management.

THE VISIBLE LEADER

Has all the features of the visible manager but fully understands the need to establish direction, align people, motivate and inspire, thus producing and sustaining change for the better. He/she transforms the organisation by transforming the people within it.

THE INVISIBLE LEADER
Is not really invisible, it's just that his/her
spirit permeates all parts of the organisation
whether they are there or not. These are Jim
Collins' Level 5 leaders who:

* Are more ambitious for their
  organisations than themselves.
* Talk about their organisation using the
  word 'our' rather than 'my'.
* Have resilience and unwavering resolve
  to make things happen.
* Are driven by an incurable need to succeed.
* Are more like plough horses than show
  horses.
* Apportion credit to others while taking the
  blame when things go wrong.
* Set up their successors in order to create
  even greater success.

Using her extensive knowledge of great leaders, Andrea went on
to describe Emmeline Pankhurst as one of the greatest invisible
leaders of all time. Yes, she had written books, but as she led the
campaign for women to be given the vote just after the turn of
the twentieth century, her public appearances had to become fewer
as she was constantly being tracked by the authorities, placing her
followers in danger of physical attack from the police. Each time
she spoke, she had to use her full command of the English language
so that her thoughts and beliefs increasingly permeated the minds
of her supporters and galvanised them into action as they strove to
become law makers rather than law breakers. In the same way, head
teachers need to ensure that their thoughts and beliefs permeate the
minds of teachers.

Brian remained silent. He periodically looked up and stared
straight into Andrea's eyes, sparkling with enthusiasm for the Spring-
gett Lane project, and he liked that. He still knew nothing of her
family which meant he had no idea where her knowledge came
from or why she was so interested in his project.

Brian knew his first challenge was to ensure that he was a visible leader and then to move forward and become an invisible leader. But he wanted respite from the conversation now. He needed to go off and think about things further, so he was glad when Andrea lightened the conversation and asked if he was seeing anybody. Brian shrugged and said, 'No, what about you?' Andrea said that, with so much travelling, it was often difficult to build a relationship, but that being on your own, moving from hotel to hotel, could be extremely lonely.

How do you put an elephant in a fridge?

Brian didn't know what to say next. The conversation was starting to become uncomfortable and Brian was feeling clumsy. He wanted to move on but just didn't know what to say, so he probably came out with the world's worst line: 'Do you use any good jokes in your training sessions?'

An awkward silence followed. Andrea filled the wine glasses, mainly for something to do while she thought, and then looked up and said, 'Well, you certainly know how to let a girl down by changing the subject! I do have three really strange questions for you that I sometimes use with my clients. You will have heard the story about how at social gatherings people always avoid talking about the elephant in the room or the one thing everybody has noticed but nobody dares comment on? Well, I want to talk about the elephant in the fridge.' Brian was now looking perplexed, so Andrea decided to cash in and reached for the notepad. She wrote:

How do you put a hippopotamus in a fridge?

Brian was now totally bemused. He reached for the notepad and simply wrote his immediate response:

God knows.

Andrea wrote:

Open the door and shove it in.
Moral: Keep leadership simple and never over-complicate it.

Andrea looked up and caught Brian's eye for a short time before clarifying what she had written. She went on to explain that when Steve Jobs returned to Apple in 1997, he found the tech company he had formed back in 1976 in a poor state of health. He said the company was making and marketing a 'zillion and one products'. His immediate task was survival and simplification. He took the range of products from over forty to just four, stating that 'simplicity is the ultimate sophistication'.[3] While Brian was thinking about this, Andrea reached for the pen once more and wrote:

> How do you put an elephant in a fridge?

Brian thought he recognised what the desired response was and grabbed the pen and wrote:

> Open the door and shove it in.

Andrea smiled, knowing she had the upper hand, and wrote:

> You can't because the hippopotamus is in there, so what will you do now?

Brian then gave his carefully considered response:

> God knows.

Andrea added her reply:

> Open the door, throw out the hippopotamus and put the elephant in.
> Moral: Get rid of stuff or systems you don't need, and do it now!

Andrea now added a third question:

> The lion is the king of the jungle and he invites all the animals to a party, but one of them fails to turn up. Which one doesn't arrive?

Brian was still puzzled by what was going on and, giving his predictable response, he wrote:

God knows.

Andrea's answer was:

It's the elephant because he is in the fridge. He is literally left out in the cold. In your school it is Anne Moody who is in the fridge, so what are you going to do about her?

It was Brian's turn again:

God knows ... so I am going to change the subject AGAIN!

And he did change the subject. He went on to tell Andrea about his thoughts on the three generations of the curriculum that existed and how we needed to move on to a fourth-generation curriculum. She listened intently and said, 'I wish you luck but I don't have much confidence.'

Why televisions will never catch on

Brian had been expecting support and encouragement and suddenly felt put down. 'Why do you say that?' he retorted.

Andrea looked up and said, 'It's down to the Bridget Driscoll factor.'

'Who on earth is Bridget Driscoll?' enquired Brian. 'Is she one of your leadership gurus?'

'No, she was the first pedestrian ever to be knocked down and killed by a motor car in the UK. The year was 1896 and the car was described by onlookers as travelling at a reckless speed, like a fire engine, and going as fast as a horse could gallop. The reality was that it was travelling at an earth shattering four miles per hour. The coroner in the case wanted motor cars taken off the road and banned forever, saying that he hoped "such a thing would never happen again". Similarly, in 1939, the *New York Times* wrote that television would never be a serious competitor for radio. If you are listening to the radio you can do other things; to watch television you have to have your eyes glued to the screen and the average American family doesn't have time for that. Decca Records told The Beatles that guitar groups were on the way out, and Tom Watson, the chairman of IBM in 1943, declared that there may be a need for five computers worldwide – and the odds are, Brian, that you have five with you at this moment in time.[4]

'The problem is that the vast majority of people don't like change and they especially don't like it in education. You already know that your secretary of state is set on having children sitting in rows, wearing blazers, with their pencils sharpened. You have come up with a brilliant concept, Brian, but only a great head teacher who is an invisible leader will bring it to fruition, and no head teacher at Springett Lane would achieve the dream while Anne Moody is left in the refrigerator. You have to become that invisible leader and let your spirit get everywhere, even to her.'

Brian looked at his watch. Time had flown and it was now nearly 11 p.m. They both knew it was time to move, but they were really enjoying each other's company. As they parted Andrea said, 'It seems to me that you still haven't formulated your views around a fourth-generation curriculum. Maybe you should think Generation Z.'

'What is Generation Z?' asked Brian.

'You had better find out what Generation Z is all about. You could start with Malala Yousafzai,' said Andrea, who kissed Brian gently on the cheek and then left.

Brian savoured the moment before he walked out into the street. After a few steps Andrea turned around and shouted, 'Brian, do you believe in Father Christmas?' Half a dozen passers-by stopped to listen for the answer.

Brian replied, 'Of course not, do you?' The answer came back, 'Of course I do. If you are going to achieve the improbable, you have to believe in the improbable. If you believe in …' but sadly Brian and the passers-by never heard the rest, as the number 52 bus roared by.

Lumpy custard at the Department for Education

Meanwhile, there was further bad news in the press for the education secretary when he was accused of mixing business with pleasure

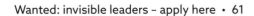

while on holiday in Marrakech. He was seen enjoying drinks with the chef behind one of the nation's leading restaurant chains. On their return, he promptly offered that chef the role of school meals adviser.[5] Metaphorical and controversial lumps were starting to appear in the custard.

Chapter 6
Books, not bullets, will change the world

Teachers to bring back old-fashioned reading tests
Daily Mail Online, 23 November 2010

Brian couldn't sleep when he got back to his apartment. He had loved his evening with Andrea. Whenever they met, he couldn't wait to meet her again. He was desperate to impress Andrea and prove that he really could transform Springett Lane. He reached for his laptop. There was perhaps just enough time to find out about Generation Z before he went to sleep. He followed Andrea's advice and started with Malala Yousafzai. Obviously he had some basic information but he felt he needed to know more. He started to read.

Malala Yousafzai was born in Mingora in Pakistan and lived in the Swat Valley. For many years her childhood was idyllic. She loved being in the classroom where she studied hard and made good progress. The school had been founded by her father, who was committed to both education and his family. The area around her home attracted tourists and its summer festivals were widely enjoyed. However, new tensions in the locality culminated in the Taliban taking control of the area. They started to attack any schools attended by girls.

Malala's bravery was evident from an early stage. In September 2008 she spoke to an audience in Peshawar and the title of her talk was 'How dare the Taliban take away my basic right to education?' At the start of 2009, Malala started blogging under a false identity about life under the Taliban and the threat to equal access to education for girls as well as boys. Later that year her identity was revealed, but not before she was named 'BBC Blogger of the Year'.

Malala knew that she was in great danger, but she continued to speak out about her right, and the right of all girls, to an education. Her bravery and activism resulted in a nomination for the International Children's Peace Prize in 2011. During the same year, she was awarded Pakistan's National Youth Peace Prize. However, Malala knew that her courage could prove costly. When she reached the age of 14, Malala learned that the Taliban had issued a death threat against both her and her family. While Malala was frightened for the safety of her father, who was an anti-Taliban activist, she believed she would be safe. She was convinced that the Taliban would not hurt a child.

Unfortunately she was wrong. On 9 October 2012, on her way home from school, a man boarded the bus on which she was travelling and demanded to know which girl was Malala. When her friends looked towards her, the man reached for his gun and fired, hitting Malala in the left side of her head. Two other girls were also injured in the bloody attack. The shooting left Malala in a critical condition, and she was flown to a military hospital in Peshawar. A portion of her skull was removed to treat her swelling brain, and to receive further care she was transferred to a hospital in Birmingham.

Thanks to the brilliance of the British medical team, Malala grew stronger. Undeterred, she continued to speak out about the importance of education, even though the fatwa against her remains. As a result of her bravery and commitment to providing education for all, in 2014 she became the youngest person ever to receive the Nobel Peace Prize. Her message is clear when she says, 'I demand of leaders we should invest in books instead of bullets.' Brian realised that Malala Yousafzai embodies everything Generation Z stands for and that they have a desire to change the world for the better.

Before long Brian found his eyes closing – Generation Z could wait until the morning. His head sank into the pillow and he drifted off to sleep, but his dreams were frightening. The images that came into his mind were of that school bus rattling along the streets of Mingora in Pakistan. There was the laughter and light-hearted conversation of the schoolgirls. Then the gunman enters, presumably looking like just another passenger. He asks a question of one of the girls, turns, looks at the innocent Malala, then bang! Brian awoke with a jolt.

Instantly he knew what his fourth-generation curriculum should look like, and some research showed him that the young people who make up Generation Z are different, want to be different and are proud to be different. The Baby Boomers, followed by the Yuppies, Generation X and the Millennials, have left their mark on the nation – and today's youngsters are not impressed. Compared to their predecessors, Generation Z are smarter and more mature. They have a desire to change the world while living a more sober lifestyle. When they look at the world's political and financial leaders they see a damaging legacy of chaos. Acts of brutal terrorism have led to innocent people being killed. Financial leaders have crippled the economy in pursuit of greed. The planet is vulnerable and potentially on the road to destruction but too many political leaders are not really prepared to fight for it. Generation Z's parents were the first in a generation of 'latchkey' kids. Many of them became saddled with debt as credit was given so readily, and as a consequence they worked excessively long hours and divorced in huge numbers. In short, Generation Z see a world in desperate need of change.

Screenagers and bloggers

With just twenty-four hours to go until the staff meeting, Brian now had a clear view about the fourth-generation curriculum at Springett Lane. It had to meet the needs of Generation Z and it had to help them change the world. As he reached for his notebook on the table he spotted the *Daily Mail* headline announcing that schools should revert to old-fashioned reading tests. He knew this was ridiculous as the young people in our schools are the first true digital natives. They are 'screenagers': the average 6-year-old may still struggle to tie shoelaces but is likely to be more technologically minded than a typical 45-year-old. Brian recalled a parent who had been told by her 8-year-old son that she shouldn't ask if he had enjoyed school today, as she would be able to find the information on his blog!

Brian started to write:

The fourth-generation curriculum	Key features
The secretary of state is wrong curriculum	We need more imaginative themes that bring high levels of engagement. Teachers should not be afraid to take unusual ideas and run with them. We should also remove the tired themes that come around year after year.
	Deeper and longer lasting learning will be achieved, and this may mean doing less better.
	The curriculum must focus on what the learners will be doing for themselves.
	There will be a greater focus on the language of learning.
	The children will become responsible citizens, imagining how their learning and acts can create a better world.
	Learning will be filled with really interesting, hard stuff.
	Children will be learning in constant collaboration with a social context.[1]

The *Daily Mail* may have wanted schools to go back to strategies that belonged in the past, but for Brian there was no turning around. Adrenalin was pumping through his veins as he decided to seek an early morning meeting with Tom at a local coffee shop.

Three-generational lessons in a fourth-generation curriculum

The hissing sound of a coffee machine in the morning can stimulate great minds. Tom and Brian were now discussing the implications of Generation Z, Brian's dream and his plan for a fourth-generation curriculum. Brian was anxious to hear what considered 'butterflies' (i.e. the small things that can make a huge difference) Tom would have to offer.

They both sipped freshly made coffee – it had the kind of bitterness that galvanised their thoughts. Tom went on to offer one of his butterflies. He told Brian that it was a good thing that he was writing his thoughts down, saying that it was important to 'think in ink' and 'talk in ink'. If you want to bring about true change, write it down so you can articulate your thoughts both to yourself and others with clarity. Brian took the hint and started to write as fast as he could. Tom began to speak and Brian knew a second butterfly was coming:

> Don't forget that most children in your school will grow up to be parents themselves, and then grandparents, and when they look back on their primary school days, they will be left with distant memories. Do you want them to remember sitting at desks preparing for tests, or do you want them to remember school and childhood as an exciting time? The butterfly I would suggest to you would be to go back and tell each member of staff to plan a three-generational lesson – the kind of lesson that they will tell their grandchildren about and most likely the kind of lesson where they feel like they are throwing away the rule book. In this nation we have become brilliant at the science of pedagogy with our learning intentions, differentiation and mini-plenaries, which are of course important. Now ask staff to focus on the art of pedagogy. Then, when that has been successful, consider asking them to plan the three-generational studies that the children will always remember – the ones that have the potential to change their lives. You have had a dream, Brian, so go back to that question and find out what Springett Lane's children are dreaming about.

The two men finished their coffees. As he left the shop, Brian glanced at the newspapers displayed on the rack. On one there was a leading article about the anniversary of Martin Luther King's 'I have a dream' speech. Brian pulled down the paper and started to

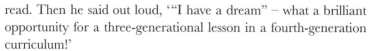

read. Then he said out loud, '"I have a dream" – what a brilliant opportunity for a three-generational lesson in a fourth-generation curriculum!'

The other customers looked up at this strange man who was talking to himself. Brian realised he had attracted some unwanted attention so added, 'Don't worry, I'm not going mad. I'm just talking to myself,' and then mumbled quietly to himself, 'and I also collect *Daily Mail* headlines.'

Each day the vision inside Brian's mind of how Springett Lane could be in the future became more and more compelling. There was now a genuine need for action. He also knew that our political masters don't necessarily like people with an educational vision and seek to deride them. Brian knew his courage would be tested.

The custard just got lumpier

You may recall that Rupert Brinton had been criticised in the press for mixing business with pleasure when he appointed a new school meals adviser. But things really started to hot up in the kitchen when a famous television chef turned his anger on the secretary of state in the press. He launched a campaign against Mr Brinton for eroding healthy school meal standards by allowing schools in his flagship academies programme to be excused from signing up to healthy food policies. The chef's ire was based on the fact that the water in schools had to be safe and the buses transporting the children to schools had to be safe, but food standards were being dangerously eroded.[2]

A short term review would have found evidence that the Department for Education was experiencing a crisis of confidence. It was on a war footing and being run like a sitcom. There were alleged complaints about bullying. Its leader was being accused of not providing young people with a rounded education. Some people were claiming that the secretary of state was mixing business with pleasure. Evidence suggested that government policies could lead to a generation of unhealthy children. Menacing storm clouds appeared to be gathering over the nation's schools.

Many might have read the articles in the press and wondered if Rupert Brinton really was a suitable person to be secretary of state for education. The prime minister clearly thought he was.

Chapter 7
People who moan about people who moan

Ban bad teachers before they start
Daily Mail Online, 25 November 2010

The morning of the staff meeting arrived and Brian was looking at a somewhat different headline from the *Daily Mail* announcing that school leaders should sack bad teachers before they start. He exclaimed out loud, 'It's a somewhat simplistic view!' He was now starting to get worried about several things. Following his exit from the coffee shop, Brian was concerned that he was increasingly talking to himself, which some people regard as a sign of madness. However, the good news was that he wasn't answering himself yet. Second, he was aware that Anne Moody was still metaphorically sitting in the refrigerator and he hadn't worked out how to get her out – or even if he wanted to get her out. Although the mental image was now making him wear a maniacal grin.

Brian was wise enough to understand what was behind the newspaper headline. It was just another example of how successive governments since the 1970s, with the support of the popular press, had developed a deliberate policy of demeaning teachers and keeping them humble. He also knew that there were teachers in the profession who should not be there because they simply weren't good enough. Nobody in their right mind would want surgery performed by an incompetent doctor, nor would they send their car to an inadequate mechanic for repairs, but every day there are parents who send their children to classrooms where the teacher can't cut the mustard.

Brian started to search the internet to discover what other exaggerated stories he could find about the profession. Wherever he turned, he seemed to find quotes from Sir Compton Urquhart, the head of Ofsted, moaning about teachers moaning, clearly making him a man of very mixed standards. He especially moaned that teachers left the car park at 3 p.m. in something that resembled the starting grid at a Grand Prix, and he also complained that they didn't understand what real pressure was.[1] This angered Brian as he knew that his own working day was regularly at least thirteen hours long and that most school car parks had vehicles in them long after 6 p.m. While Brian thought that Her Majesty's Chief Inspector of Schools was out of touch, he was now having serious doubts about how he should conduct that evening's professional development meeting. He wondered if he should change the nature of the staff meeting and not start with the questions from *Who Wants To Be a Millionaire?* They had seemed like a good idea at the time but now they just felt stupid. He knew there were serious recruitment and retention problems with teaching staff, especially in schools like Springett Lane, but maybe the meeting should be about applying real pressure and seeking to bring about his changes by telling the staff that they were simply not good enough.

The digital clock clicked to 6.30 a.m. and he wanted to ring Andrea for guidance, but it seemed too early. He showered, dressed and then risked it, ringing at 7 a.m. Half an hour later it was time for another early morning coffee meeting. The two of them were sitting with lattes and freshly baked croissants. Brian had printed out the Chief Inspector of School's claims that teachers didn't understand what real pressure was and passed them to Andrea, who read them and announced that, from a leadership stance, they were downright foolish and destructive and could cause unimaginable damage. She pointed out, too, that it would be equally damaging for Brian to suggest to the staff that they weren't good enough. It was her view that our greatest leaders did not bury themselves in negativity but had boundless optimism. It was high morale and self-esteem that would be essential in bringing in three-generational lessons within a fourth-generation curriculum, and allowing Generation Z to flourish and make a significant difference to the world. She reminded him of all the press reports about how morale in the teaching profession was damaged by the words of politicians and the press, and encouraged him to focus on finding new ways of doing things and to allow success to breed success.

Another way of doing things: *The Happy Manifesto*

Andrea then suggested Brian went to his computer to look up Henry Stewart's *The Happy Manifesto* and use it first as a key strategy for the staff development meeting that evening and then specifically for a conversation with Anne Moody.[2] Then she handed Brian a memory stick and told him to watch a brief clip from the film *Invictus* before the meeting because it would give him strength and allow him to approach it in the right manner. Breakfast club came and went, as did the morning briefing. By 10 a.m. Brian had checked out *The Happy Manifesto* and was writing in his notebook once more:[3]

1. Trust your people: step out of approval. Instead, pre-approve and focus on supporting your people.
2. Make your people feel good: make this a focus of management.
3. Give freedom within clear guidelines: people want to know what is expected of them but they want the freedom to find the best way to achieve their goals.
4. Be open and transparent: more information means people can take responsibility and ownership.
5. Recruit for attitude, train for skill: instead of qualifications and experience, recruit on attitude and potential ability.
6. Celebrate mistakes: create a truly no-blame culture to enable people to innovate without fear.
7. Community: create mutual benefit, have a positive impact on the world and build your organisation too.
8. Love work, get a life: the world, and your job, needs you well rested, well nourished and well supported.
9. Select managers who are good at managing: make sure your people are supported by somebody who is good at doing just that, and find other routes for those whose strengths lie elsewhere. Even better, allow people to choose their managers.
10. Play to your strengths: make sure your people spend most of their time doing what they are good at.

While Brian was continuing to anticipate the staff meeting with a sense of fear and trepidation, he also knew that he had to appear outwardly confident to create a sense of energy and purpose. He had to exude success and make the staff optimistic about the changes he was proposing.

He shouldn't have worried. While a lack of self-confidence can strike any leader, the best ones will close their eyes, count to ten and move on. Worry is a negative energy that is a depressing waste of time. Brian's fear was misguided, because if there is one thing a school leader can do to create a sense of purpose it is to talk with passion about the things they truly believe in. It is even more potent if they add a few highly tentative, speculative questions. Brian had five in his notebook which he was going to use straight after the *Who Wants To Be a Millionaire?* questions. As he stood up to leave the room, he looked down and saw Andrea's memory stick which he had forgotten about.

Great leaders are great simplifiers

Brian quickly pushed the memory stick into his computer and the computer loaded the clip from *Invictus*. It showed images of Nelson Mandela arriving at the government offices on his first day as president of South Africa. He was looking dismayed because people were packing their cases, boxes and bags, ready to leave. They knew they were the employees of the previous regime, and therefore assumed their work was now at an end. They were scurrying around, collecting their possessions because they feared imminent reprisals. Mandela asked if all the staff who were still there could come and meet him immediately. They collected in a room, filled with suspicion, fear and trepidation, expecting that the new president wanted the satisfaction of firing them himself.

The hairs on the back of Brian's neck stood up as the scene unfolded. As Mandela walked down the aisle he paused to greet people and to thank them for coming to see him at short notice.

Then when he reached the front he turned to speak to them. It was as though a message of peace and reconciliation was coming from his eyes, which were glinting as he spoke. He informed those present that if they wanted to leave their employment then that was fine, but went on to say that if they thought they had to leave because of their language, or the colour of their skin, or because of who they worked for previously then they should think again. After a pause he went on to state clearly that the past belongs in the past and it was time to look to the future. Nelson Mandela called on all those present in the room to stay and work together in partnership using their considerable abilities to build a new South Africa that would be a shining light in the world.[4]

In fewer than 300 words, Nelson Mandela had embraced and endorsed Stewart's *The Happy Manifesto* and totally changed the atmosphere in a previously hostile room.

Every leader gets just one chance to make a first impression, and in those few moments Mandela made sure he grabbed it and created maximum impact. In that brief address, there was a vision being articulated and disseminated to every person present. Nelson Mandela was aware of the need to take every strategic step he could to achieve his vision, and to do so he needed to create a culture where everybody felt they could achieve, had a duty to achieve and had a duty to help others achieve.

Once the questions from *Who Wants To Be a Millionaire?* had been answered, Brian was going to focus on why he had asked the questions in the first place. The answer was written boldly and clearly in his notebook, for this was to be the title of the staff development meeting:

If knowledge is available at the touch of a button, then what should schools be about?

Brian reflected on the discussion points he had written down to steer the meeting. He realised that he had continually used the word 'I', but then he reflected on Andrea's message on invisible leadership. He had recently got into the bad habit of using phrases like 'my school' and 'my teachers' which made him seem like an autocrat. He knew that whatever progress was made from here on, all those connected with the school needed to be able to say, 'We did it, and we did it ourselves.'

However, before asking the questions he told the staff of his dream about Malala Yousafzai and how she reflected everything Generation Z stood for. He told the story with great skill; the audience listened intently. Some of them gasped audibly as Brian told of the bullet being fired. There was now an emotional hook into everything that followed. There is a part of the brain called the limbic system that triggers such emotional responses. Brian didn't know this. He was simply working intuitively. He knew that he wanted the school to meet the needs of the children growing up as Generation Z. A series of questions formed in his mind:

1. If information is available at the touch of a button, then what is it that our school really needs to provide for the Springett Lane community?
2. What would we need to do if, collectively, we wanted to transform the way in which children learn in our school?
3. How can we give children a truly remarkable education that equips them for life in the twenty-first century?
4. What would we need to do if, collectively, we were to become the most creative and inspirational teachers this school has ever seen?
5. The secretary of state thinks children learn best seated in rows and learning the names of the kings and queens of England, but do we really think he is right?

After a tentative start, the meeting went well and contributions flowed. Sometimes tensions emerged but soon a consensus started to develop that the curriculum was no longer fit for purpose. Both teachers and children had become tired of the recycled themes that came around year after year, none of which helped the children to develop as responsible citizens with a desire to change the world for the better. The teachers were becoming animated and heart rates rose. There was much arm waving and wagging of fingers. However, Anne Moody did not join in. She remained motionless with her handbag on her knees and her fingers tightly clenched around the straps. She was hunched up and looked uncomfortable. In fact, it was rather as though she really had been crammed into a cold, dark refrigerator. Brian wondered if the door would open and the light come on anytime soon.

Although Brian had noted Anne Moody's demeanour, he had more immediate problems. While there was enthusiastic and passionate dialogue, it was scattergun and there was a need to make coherent sense of it. People were eagerly making contributions but nothing was being recorded. He knew he had to intervene if he was going to be able to achieve a successful high impact conclusion. Just then his mobile phone vibrated on the table in front of him. A message flashed up from Andrea. 'Good God!' thought Brian to himself. 'She must be a hell of a good leadership consultant. She even knows what's happening when she isn't in the room.'

The message simply read:

> 'Great leaders are almost always great simplifiers who can cut through argument, debate and doubt, to offer a solution everybody can understand.' Colin Powell
> Tell them they can only use six words each.
> Andrea xx
> P.S. Wine bar tonight?

Andrea had provided Brian with a flash of inspiration. Legend has it that Ernest Hemingway, in addition to his many fine novels, wrote the following six word story: 'For sale: baby shoes, never worn.' Brian was also sure he had read that six words were the fewest that could be used to write a complete story. He drew himself up and took control, telling the staff that time was rapidly running out and there was a need to consider the next steps. He challenged those present to capture the spirit of their comments in just six words, but they also had to be six words which encapsulated the richness of the English language and had the potential to make the hairs tingle on the back of the neck.

The whole atmosphere changed. Silence descended and Brian feared he had killed the enthusiasm, but he was also prepared to wait. Then the contributions started coming and Brian scribbled them down:

> Engage the heart, engage the brain.
> Make it real, relevant and rich.

The curriculum: a voyage of discovery.
Inspiration and aspiration change the world.
Out with recycled, in with real.

Brian started to feel as though he had achieved a mandate for his plans. He felt that at the next meeting they could move on to his 'I Have a Dream' project. The room then fell quiet again. It was Anne Moody who spoke next. 'Can I just say something?' she asked. Brian felt a sense of dismay. He knew the spirit of the whole meeting now hung in the balance. He was really tempted to say, 'No, I think it's time to wrap up now.' However, as he opened his mouth to utter those words, he found himself saying the exact opposite. Instead he said, 'Go ahead, the floor is yours,' while in his head he was saying, 'Drat, drat, drat, what on earth have I done now?'

Anne Moody then offered a series of six word stories of her own. Brian found himself writing them down:

The senses play a critical role.
Emotional engagement is central to learning.
Rich authentic experiences make memorable learning.
Communication and expression go beyond writing.
Positivity breeds success, threats breed negativity.
Thinking and challenge equals positive impact.

In thirty-six words Anne Moody had captured the spirit of the meeting. Not only that, she had summarised the key findings of the last twenty years of neuroscience for teachers.

Brian was lost for words, but knew he had to say something. His next sentence was very clumsy. 'But what do we do about Rupert Brinton who says that children learn best sitting at desks in rows?'

Anne Moody spoke again. 'Well, that's easy … teach them outdoors!'

A few nervous giggles followed and then total silence.

You can't – the fields have been sold!

Even if it had been possible to teach children outdoors, the chances of using school grounds were diminishing in many schools. And this meant further bad news for the secretary of state for education. The press turned on him for the way in which he had overseen the selling off of school playing fields. One newspaper commented, 'We are accustomed to his wilful ignorance and breathtaking arrogance, but his response to the 150,000 people who signed an online petition protesting at his plans to allow schools to reduce the size of their playing fields beggared belief. "I admire their passion but they are wrong," he said.'[5]

Chapter 8
Six $1.5 million words

Today, children, we're going on a trip ... to the playground: claim culture means teachers are scared to leave the premises

Daily Mail Online, 8 September 2012

'Well, if you ask me she belongs in a fridge and she should be left there!' Brian said to Andrea as they sipped their wine. He had just described the absurdity of Anne Moody's sarcastic 'teach them outdoors' comment. However, he didn't quite get the response he had been expecting.

'Just hang on a moment,' said Andrea, 'and go back to Anne Moody's six word stories.' Andrea knew that too many businesses and enterprises produce bulky policy statements, long term plans and procedural guidance notes. In the hurly-burly of a busy working day, such documents are quickly tossed aside or forgotten, whereas six words can keep an employee focused, particularly if they clearly spell out the direction the organisation is taking. She also believed that too many of our managers simply produce documents that cover their own backs. She added that it goes back to the difference between managers and leaders, and reminded Brian that the evidence tells us that our best leaders keep it simple.

Andrea reached for her pen. She said that the political leaders of Nevada had recently paid US$9 million for these six powerful words that captured the spirit of the state for advertising purposes:

A world within. A state apart.[1]

And that equates to US$1.5 million per word. Andrea continued to write down other six word slogans:

> Between love and madness lies Obsession. (Calvin Klein)
> Engineered to move the human spirit. (Mercedes-Benz)
> More experience than our name suggests. (Virgin Atlantic)

With a glint in her eye, Andrea said, 'The last one is my favourite.' She then continued with, 'How do you know Anne Moody's comment was sarcastic? Her other thoughts were positive and, besides, why *not* teach them outdoors? Our most successful businesses have a unique selling point – something that makes them stand out from the rest. Schools should have the same. If I had children, I would love them to spend time on outdoor learning, it just feels right. Wasn't it something that Mr Chipping was prone to do in the classic novel *Goodbye, Mr Chips*, and it seemed to work for him.'[2]

Tadpoles taste gritty and are difficult to bite

Andrea was on a roll and was now telling Brian that tadpoles taste 'gritty and they are difficult to bite because they slip around on the tongue' and that while they don't have a distinctive taste, they can be 'slightly moreish' because you search out the flavour. For once, Brian felt repulsed by what Andrea was saying. She could tell this and continued, 'If you don't know what tadpoles taste like then you should. In fact, all young people should get a jam jar to catch some tadpoles and then get a spoon and sacrifice a couple.'

Brian grimaced and said, 'Do you really believe that?'

'No,' responded Andrea, 'but naturalist and broadcaster Chris Packham does. He says that eating a couple of tadpoles might instil a passion for the outdoor world in young people. I read it in a newspaper.'[3]

Andrea continued to talk: 'Recently I was on the phone to my brother in America, and he told me a story. A few years ago he moved with his wife and son, Josh, to a new housing estate that had been carefully designed by the planners to ensure that children could play and roam around with a degree of safety. And that is what the children did. Josh and his mates built dens, they built dams and floated home-made boats in the stream that ran along the edge of the estate. In short, their imaginations became their entertainment. They made ramps to ride their bikes and skateboards over the stream and sometimes they made cycle speedways or replayed great games of baseball. However, before long, storm clouds gathered. The planners moved away and people banded together into a residents' association that started to set rules that would restrict play. The ramps were removed and the dens cleared away, and pristine and well-cultivated lawns took their place. After that, Game Boys and SEGA became the children's playthings and, before long, the health authorities had a childhood obesity problem on their hands.'[4]

Brian joined in: 'It's not just a problem in the United States.' He went on to tell Andrea about an article he had read about a group of girls building a den in Warkworth Woods during their Easter holidays. 'They were having great fun, chatting, laughing and giggling, watching their den take shape, until some dog walkers reported them for antisocial behaviour. One of the girl's parents had said that dog walkers had complained about the den builders dragging branches around. Originally, their parents had all been delighted when their daughters announced they were going to build a den. The activity seemed so much better than roaming the streets or staring at a mobile phone. The parents were then astounded by the police cars that came screeching to a halt and the officers who leapt out of them ready to investigate the incident. The girls, who had been taking photographs of their new den, suddenly froze, feeling terrified, as the police arrived. They had no alcohol or drugs or loud music, just some fizzy drinks and crisps. A short while after the incident, the police confirmed that no further action was deemed to be necessary.'[5]

Brian went quiet. All of a sudden, the absolute importance of outdoor education had become clear. Andrea was uneasy about the silence and asked, 'Is everything all right?' 'Outdoor learning could be the answer,' exclaimed Brian, who then, on impulse, kissed Andrea on the cheek. After the initial surprise, Andrea composed herself and said, 'I think I mentioned outdoor learning first, but thanks for the kiss. I'm not opposed to you kissing me, but can you warn me before you do that again! I might need to prepare myself better,' and then instantly regretted making the comment.

Everything was certainly all right. Indeed, it suddenly felt better than that. Brian's brain was working overtime. He had glazed over because he was trying to recall a piece of research from a distant corner of his mind. He reached for his notebook as he recalled the work about 'containerised kids' produced by Glasgow University. He wrote down the key elements of the research and then added a final comment.[6]

Too often from a very early age children are containerised:

* They are strapped into recliners and placed in front of the television.
* They are strapped into car seats.
* They are strapped into buggies as their parents stroll or jog in the park.
* The project electronically tagged 3-year-olds and found many were only physically active for twenty minutes per day.
* While children are given access to learning outdoors in the foundation stage, this is too quickly taken away and they become containerised in the classroom, just where the secretary of state wants them to be – sitting in rows.

Brian knew that further research was needed, but he also recognised that Anne Moody's comment had inadvertently taken him to a new level of thinking. Increasing the amount of time the children spent learning outdoors was rapidly becoming a key element in his plan. He scribbled down three key names as a prompt for later: Friedrich Froebel, Rudolf Steiner and Maria Montessori. He wondered what Ofsted would think if his plan was inked in for future reference. Clearly Brian had remembered to think in ink.

Brian already knew that the days of doing things because it was deemed that Ofsted would approve were behind him. He also knew he would have battles with the staff. However, he had a sneaking suspicion that there was a long forgotten Ofsted report into the

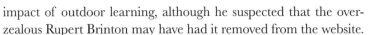

impact of outdoor learning, although he suspected that the over-zealous Rupert Brinton may have had it removed from the website.

Brian's brain was pulsing with energy. He knew he had read a news-paper story about over 100 housing estates in the north of England with 'no ball games' signs. Planning permission to erect basketball posts had received objections because there was a fear that it would attract children, and a parish council had even dealt with a complaint about a child cycling down the pavement – the issue being that their bike wheels squeaked. Then, to compound matters further, Brian looked out of the wine bar window and straight at a sign saying, 'District Council bye-law. The use of skateboards in this area is prohibited.' The spirit of Oscar Wilde's great children's story, *The Selfish Giant*, was not confined to stopping children experiencing rich activities in a fantasy garden in the skies. It was alive and kicking in every corner of twenty-first century Britain. And, to make matters worse, it was happening at a time when obesity levels were rising and scientists were complaining about young people suffering from nature-deficit disorder.

Be known for your footprints and not your fingerprints

Brian pushed the notepad towards Andrea saying, 'If I want the children to spend more time learning outdoors, then give me the structures to bring my dream to reality.'

Andrea picked up the pen and wrote.

The three pillars of successful innovation:

Dialogue: Take every opportunity to speak about your plans, both formally and informally, until everybody is talking to each other in the same way and sharing ideas and successes and even problems.

Modelling: Don't be afraid to roll up your sleeves and lead from the front. Use others to model best practice or consider peer coaching/mentoring schemes.

Keep reviewing and evaluating and offering the 'tweak of the week'. Tell people what you enjoyed seeing this week and what you hope to see next week.

Andrea offered an explanation: 'You need to get dialogue into the psyche of the organisation. The only way to do this is to articulate the plan with belief and passion on every possible occasion until dialogue about the initiative is taking place daily in every nook and cranny of the school. Second, you seek out good practice and use it to model your dream and, when necessary, take the initiative by leading from the front, while others view the impact of your work. Finally, you walk around the school, joining in the outdoor lessons or the subsequent follow-ups back in the classroom, and you offer feedback to individuals and teams. Then you tell them what you like about their work and how you would like them to tweak their work in the short term. Your friend Tom would call this butterfly strategy "The tweak of the week". It's about finding those slight changes that will have a significant impact across the whole organisation.'

'Is that Henry Stewart's *The Happy Manifesto* in action?' asked Brian.

Andrea agreed it was, and then asked about the names that Brian had written in his notebook and why he had done so. Two minutes later, after a second bottle of wine had been opened, Andrea's iPhone was in action and Brian had completed his notes.

Friedrich Froebel (1782–1852)	Believed that children learn best when close to nature, making connections between themselves and the wider world in order to understand their place and role within it. They learn to become responsible for their world and to look after each other. He was against learning being compartmentalised into subjects. Children learn extensively outdoors through rich activities with quieter places provided for calm and reflection. Froebel introduced the term kindergarten (garden for children).

Rudolf Steiner (1861–1925)	Made links between a child's spirituality and their world and wanted to create a way of learning that developed children's cognitive and social skills in secure and calm environments. He encouraged creative thought, self-led play, risk taking and the use of the senses. The children developed a respect for each other and their environment and a trust in their own judgement and abilities. There was a tremendous emphasis on the outdoor environment in spaces that were as natural as possible, some of which were covered so the children could escape the elements as they were encouraged to explore in all seasons. There are significant similarities between the approach and today's 'forest schools'.
Maria Montessori (1870–1952)	Wanted children to be released from the shackles of a formal education system in order to learn essential life skills and explore the world using all their senses. She pioneered the links between indoor and outdoor learning. Children select activities within a limited range to take learning forward. Repetition was seen as important to ensure learning became embedded. There is much evidence that, intuitively, Montessori's methods link well to what we now know about how the brain develops.

It was clear to Brian that, over a period of two centuries, these three pioneers of outdoor education had developed thinking that needed to be applied in the current education system. They had left a legacy that was precisely what Generation Z was looking for, and Brian knew that it was his job to help young people discover that legacy by rekindling its spirit.

'It's all about legacy,' Brian murmured to himself. But Andrea responded, 'And that's what leaders do when they plan their legacy. They think about what will remain in their school long after they have departed, and about the influence they seek to have on those who work with them.'

Leaving a legacy was just what Brian had in mind. He wanted to create a tradition of high quality experiential primary education at Springett Lane. While there were clear differences in the approaches of the esteemed educationalists, they all wanted similar outcomes for children: independence, decision making, social awareness and a sense of being a part of their environment and creating a better world, rather than just being an onlooker. All of them recognised the need for outdoor education with children learning in both natural and man-made environments. Children were encouraged to be risk takers and to learn through adventurous, imaginative, hands-on activities. These were Brian's ideals too.

As a nation, we have moved towards safer and more sterile learning environments. Brian remembered a *Daily Mail* headline which stated that teachers had become afraid to leave their premises because of the threat of legal action in the event of an accident. This made that trip to the playground a special treat rather than the norm. Maybe our anxieties about our children are becoming detrimental to their welfare and education. The question was, 'Should we be more like our predecessors and be bold and brave enough to break out and do what we truly believe to be right, or is the secretary of state right and children do need to be sitting in rows?' However, his concerns about Ofsted remained unanswered. Brian didn't know which way to turn. He took another sip of wine.

'Here you go,' said Andrea, who had been researching on her mobile phone. 'A report from Ofsted on learning outside the classroom.' She picked up the pen and wrote down the key messages:[7]

* Memorable experiences led to memorable learning.
* The place where learning takes place added to the value.
* Learning outside the curriculum contributed to children staying safe.
* Learning outside the curriculum included and benefitted all groups (especially the underachieving) and hands-on experience in a range of locations contributed much to improvements in achievement, standards, motivation, personal development and behaviour for all pupils.

So Anne Moody had been right all along. Brian still didn't know if her comments were meant to be ridiculous or profound. In reality, it turned out to be the latter. Both Andrea and Brian sank back into their chairs with their eyes closed. After the flurry of adrenalin-pumping excitement, they both needed to collect their thoughts.

They finished their wine, talking of this and that, until it was time to leave, when Brian kissed Andrea. She was smiling as they got up from the table, but just as they started to head off in their different directions, Andrea suddenly refocused her attention, turned and said, 'Remember these three words, Brian: anonymity, irrelevance and immeasurability.' Then, after another pause, she added, 'And you have just kissed me again without giving me any warning!'

'Sorry,' said Brian.

'I'm not,' said Andrea. 'And remember, I believe in Father Christmas, even if you don't.'

Brian had no idea what she meant and headed back to his apartment feeling a little confused about his emotions.

Hanging upside down on monkey bars

Brian was still contemplating the three words when he arrived home and thought back to what he had written in his notebook earlier. He knew that he now had to start to stand out from the rest and not simply be an anonymous, easily forgotten head teacher. In order to be a truly inspirational leader, he had to do the things he believed in and not things that felt irrelevant to him. Finally, he had to find a way of measuring what he was achieving. Overall, Brian was feeling invigorated, although he still had a sense of trepidation. It was just at that moment that an email pinged in from Eve:

> Hi Bri,
>
> I think your Brinton bloke has an ally out here in the US. The superintendent of schools in Atlanta has just banned playtime, saying, 'We are intent on improving academic performance. You don't do that by having kids hanging upside down on monkey bars.' Strange old world, Bri, most of the big employers out here on the sunny west coast believe an element of play increases productivity.[8]
>
> Eve x

And that removed the trepidation. He knew he had to find the strength to move forward with his plans.

A second email quickly followed:

> P.S. Brian,
> If play is important for adults, why don't you come out here and play with me?
> Eve x

Has-beens and never have-beens

There was now even more reason for Brian to question the competence of his political masters and the agencies they operate, as once more Rupert Brinton found himself in stormy waters. At a conference he had spoken about his team of gifted Ofsted inspectors. The trouble was that many head teachers did not feel confident that the inspection process was working fairly. Others considered the process to be downright destructive. Many school leaders thought that the inspectors ranged from inadequate to outstanding, just as schools did. Others considered that the inspectors were not especially gifted but more like 'has-beens' or 'never have-beens'. An article in the *TES* reflected some of these concerns. Head teachers had asked for more background information on the inspectors in order that schools could judge the ability of the inspection team. This was refused, making Ofsted and the Department for Education appear out of touch with reality. Reports suggested that you had a greater chance of a successful complaint against Ryanair than Ofsted.[9]

However, even more concerning were the accusations of bias at the Department for Education when they were accused of giving advance notice of inspections to the government's preferred academy chains. This obviously gave such schools an unfair advantage and then allowed the government to claim their initiatives were a clear success. Brian could imagine the Chief Inspector reading the article and starting to moan.[10]

Chapter 9
The three signs of a miserable job

Church school head sacked ageing teachers 'to replace them with busty young women'

Daily Mail Online, 25 September 2009

When Andrea told Brian to remember the three words, anonymity, irrelevance and immeasurability, she had been referring to a previous conversation with Brian based on *The Three Signs of a Miserable Job* by Patrick Lencioni. The book argued that, when somebody was unhappy in their work (and surely Anne Moody was), there were three main reasons for their dismay. First, they felt invisible when their contribution was not recognised or valued. Second, they felt the work they were doing was not in line with their value system, therefore it felt irrelevant. Third, they were in desperate need of finding a system of measuring their success in order that small achievable steps would eventually lead to larger strides.[1] While Brian understood the theory that Andrea had explained, he still held the view that Anne Moody simply wasn't good enough and that she could prove to be a thorn in his side. However, he had decided to speak to her at the end of the following day.

Brian gazed at the *Daily Mail* headline which told of a head teacher replacing 'ageing teachers' with 'busty young women'. He considered that the headline was most likely misleading and probably hid a whole range of facts. Maybe the truth was that the teachers being replaced were either not of an appropriate standard or had failed to move with the times; therefore, the school had rightly recruited younger, more energetic and more flexible members of staff. Though the new teachers may well have been attractive, this would surely have been irrelevant to the selection process.

Brian had rightly chosen not to ask Anne Moody to come to his room. While he knew he wanted to confront certain aspects of her overall conduct and classroom practice, he didn't want the meeting to be excessively confrontational. He went into her classroom, convinced that Anne Moody's 'teach them outdoors' comment had been a devious swipe at his leadership and his vision for a new Springett Lane Primary School.

'But I meant it!' Anne Moody insisted when Brian had clumsily gone on to the attack. The silence that followed allowed Brian time to think and drink in the atmosphere of what was a quite depressing learning environment. The working walls that were allegedly there to support current learning objectives had not changed since the start of the school year. They were now no better than yellowing stale wallpaper, unnoticed by anyone who entered the room. There were some bits and pieces of the children's work displayed in one corner, but the colours around it were so vivid they would have detracted from the potential quality of the work. However, it was less Blue Flag and more Blue Peter as the children had all dutifully followed a prescribed set of instructions to produce thirty almost identical pieces of work.

Brian's problem was that he was not working in his normal way. He had gone into the meeting to confront a situation and had found himself becoming increasingly assertive, whereas normally he would have tried to negotiate and influence people to reach a mutually agreed conclusion. In short, he would have been wise to remember Henry Stewart's *The Happy Manifesto*. Unfortunately, his next comment was even clumsier: 'But you never do anything exciting with these children and you never take them outside. You don't really mean it!'

As the tension mounted, Anne Moody went for fight when many others would have gone for flight. From somewhere deep inside her she summoned up her long lost passions and beliefs: 'The trouble is, Mr Smith, that I *do* mean it, but I am not sure that you do. There have been a string of head teachers who have come into this school and spoken about the values of an idealistic child-centred education where children learn through the tightly focused rich sensory experiences we create. They speak of discovery methods, the arts and how teachers must develop a sense of awe, wonder and spirituality in children, but then promptly set up structures to test the children every half term of every year. We are told to follow the national frameworks with the children in the morning and fill their minds with potentially useless information in the afternoon, although some of it may be useful for a pub quiz.

'However, children will not grow up recognising the sound of a robin singing, or the names of trees, or appreciating the beauty of wild flowers coming into bloom. Nor will they have the emotional intelligence to overcome the significant challenges that lie ahead of them in a rapidly changing world. Instead, the children attend after-school booster classes and revision courses rather than being Cubs and Scouts, climbing trees or jumping on the stepping stones across a river. It is as though there are four curricula in this nation: the *ideal curriculum* which we all know is the right one for our children, and the *official curriculum* which can be derived from the nationally prescribed courses. Then there is the *real curriculum* which is based on what actually happens in the classroom. Some schools create rich, memorable learning experiences for the children in their care, and those children thrive as they develop new knowledge, skills and attitudes which lead to deep understanding. By contrast, in too many classrooms the teachers are frightened by the constant accountability. In such classes these worries lead to unimaginative teaching, and there is a genuine fear of letting the children express themselves in a more creative way. Finally, there is the *hidden curriculum* which consists of the messages that the children really receive about learning and whether or not they and their efforts are truly valued. The true purpose of a curriculum should not be to cover but uncover.

'In too many of our schools, children experience the same old tired and safe topics time and again. Lessons take place in safe, sterile learning environments where they are taught as though they are undergraduates rather than 7- or 9-year-olds. Some teachers, and I have been one of them, are scared to do the things they really believe in, and others haven't even decided what they believe in because they are just used to being told what to do. When I asked my 11-year-old nephew if he was scared about the SATs test, he told me that he wasn't but his teachers were. And that's me, Mr Smith, I am scared.

'We need bold head teachers, Mr Smith, but most of the heads who have passed through this school have been anonymous figures, doing a job which seemed irrelevant to their beliefs, and who only knew how to measure their successes through test outcomes. Mr Smith, I suspect when the pressure for results really mounts, you will be scared too and therefore no better than the rest.'

Brian thought, 'Good heavens, has she read Lencioni's *The Three Signs of a Miserable Job* too?' Regrettably, his reaction was to be silent while he thought about what had just been said.

Eventually Anne Moody broke the silence and said, 'Well, maybe if we are both scared then perhaps we both need to be bolder. You see, Mr Smith, I know that you really want me out of this place because you think I am being obstructive. You may succeed, but I won't go down without a fight because maybe, and it is maybe, I know more about the best primary education than you do.'

There seemed to be little else to say. Brian made a more thoughtful response this time saying, 'Let's both think further and talk again tomorrow.'

Brian returned to his room mumbling under his breath. He was both angry and confused. He certainly wasn't happy with Anne Moody's classroom practice, which certainly didn't match the things she said she believed in. Most surprising of all was that she seemed to agree with most of what Brian was seeking to achieve. Brian had gone expecting to lay down his expectations and maybe achieve a moral victory, but left feeling that he had received a telling off. He also realised that he had been accused of creating a culture of fear. It now felt as though lightning bolts were shooting out from his forehead. Those who saw him walking down the corridor towards them quickly rerouted, fearing his anger could be directed at them. Teachers huddled in corners asking, 'What's the matter with the boss?' Others described it as a colourful moment in his career. His face was bright red, his temper was black and his language was blue.

However, the reality was that Brian had learned a great deal and knew he had things to write down in his notebook. He wanted to capture the messages of Anne Moody's different layers of the curriculum. However, what he didn't realise was that she had learned a great deal too. But let's focus on Brian first as he tried to capture the spirit of Anne Moody's comments about the curriculum in a simple diagram. It appeared to him that there were definitely two routes, and if he was to truly leave a legacy it needed to be route 2.

Route 1
(Safe and sound with possible moderate gains)

Route 2
(High risk strategies but could have high dividends)

The ideal curriculum
Where the passionate beliefs of school leaders are manifest in all the school does

The official curriculum
Planning that starts from nationally prescribed documents

The official curriculum
Is added into thinking as a secondary form of planning

The real curriculum
Is built from the official curriculum: master classes, revision courses and booster classes provide short term gains in progress and attainment

The real curriculum
Takes account of the national curriculum but with imaginative high impact teaching and themes

The hidden negative curriculum
Where children see education as preparing for and passing tests dominated by closed tasks and safe teaching

The hidden positive curriculum
Where education contributes to a magical childhood and children achieve in a wide variety of contexts

Brian added in the scales as the final part of the diagram. He had read Malcolm Gladwell's brilliant book *The Tipping Point* in which he argues that, when any initiative is implemented with rigour and passion, a point will be reached when any final strands of resistance disintegrate and new practice and procedures are fully implemented.[2] Brian had grown tired of playing safe and to others' rules. A new and different type of leader was emerging. Potentially this was going to be a voyage of discovery that could lead his children to very different and exciting places. It would be a transformed Brian who next spoke to Anne Moody.

Thank you for the music and goodbye!

This was a line from an article in *The Guardian*. It is not very often that a politician's plans elicit an angry response from a cellist. However, that is how Julian Lloyd Webber responded to the government's National Plan for Music, which advised local authorities to cease providing funding for music services. The press considered that the likely outcome would be that music tuition would now be for the middle classes only. Julian Lloyd Webber commented, 'This consultation must be aborted if we are to realise our dream that every child should have access to music.'[3] This cellist was certainly taking up his bow in anger. It was an indication that more and more people were becoming concerned about whether the government were capable of leading an education system in which a wide range of talents are developed. Anne Moody had rightly said that the purpose of the curriculum was not to cover but to uncover. The question was how many potential musicians would now never have their talents uncovered. The unrest around government policies was growing.

Chapter 10

When teachers learn from each other, their future will be secured

Teacher shortage reaching crisis levels

Daily Mail Online, 1 February 2014

It was 5 p.m. and the anger and adrenalin from the showdown with Anne Moody were seeping away when Tom wandered in. He was genuinely interested in Brian's project and loved to call in for updates, but on this occasion he was more worried about his well-being. He looked at the despondent Brian and said, 'Penny for them?' The response from our beleaguered school leader was, 'Tom, you wouldn't want to know my thoughts because you would be dismayed by my ineptitude and walk away in disgust.'

'I doubt it,' said Tom. 'I was a head for thirteen years and cannot believe the mistakes I made. For each of those years I managed to convince the local authority I was a *new* head.'

After listening to the story of Brian's meeting with Anne Moody, Tom rubbed his bristly cheek (because he had once again forgotten to shave) and gave his considered response. 'Successive governments and the so-called popular press have brought our wonderful profession to its knees. As a result, a third of teachers have considered career changes and 25% of new teachers leave the profession within four years. Even Ofsted is now expressing concerns that we have a brain drain of teachers who are flocking abroad to work.[1] Too often we just let these people slip away because we have underdeveloped views about staff retention in education. Time after time, those in the profession give a clear message that society needs to place greater value on the work of teachers. The government refuse to listen because they think they can solve the problem simply by paying small amounts of incentive money at the point when a teacher shortage arrives. Then, when they believe they have made the situation secure, the government, the inspectorate and the media can bring them to their knees all over again.'

Brian looked up and said desperately, 'It's going to take more than a butterfly to correct that one.'

'No, just common sense,' said Tom, 'and then the butterflies will do their job.' He continued, 'Look, schools are in the business of learning, but it is at the point where teachers and schools start learning from each other within a partnership of equals that future success and staff contentment is assured. I am glad that Anne Moody is fighting for her future. You need to find the structures that will enable you and others to invest your considerable expertise and intellectual capital in her, rather than leaving her in that proverbial refrigerator or tossing her onto the scrapheap. If you want to grow butterflies, try this for an idea – magnets of excellence.'

It was turning dark outside and driving rain was beating against the windowpanes. It was now 5.30 p.m. and Brian was hungry and desperate for the sanctuary of his apartment. While it would have been tempting to suggest leaving this conversation for another time, he decided to let Tom continue. Almost unconsciously he started to write:

What most teachers want that governments will never provide:

* To feel proud because they feel engaged in developing exciting, innovative and successful practice that will improve a young person's life chances.
* To come to a school that has self-belief and a can-do culture.
* Collaborative leadership aimed at developing excellent primary practice.
* A sense that they and every other member of staff have good practice worthy of wider dissemination.

Brian retorted, 'It sounds like Henry Stewart's *The Happy Manifesto* all over again.'

Tom continued, 'You're right, it does link to *The Happy Manifesto*. Indeed, it starts to provide a structure for it. You're determined to do things differently. Well, the dreaded Brinton is obsessed with the so-called strong schools taking over those that are deemed to be coasting, although he doesn't seem able to adequately define the term coasting. Michael Fullan said that "At the point when teachers learn from each other, their future will be secured."[2] Rupert Brinton thinks that a teacher's professional development should primarily come through his "teaching schools", and the model is a sensible one. However, here is an even more sensible idea: why not create a teaching school within your own school? Don't bother with accreditation and form-filling because that is just a draining waste of time. It is simply a bureaucratic way of making schools jump through hoops. Just use your energy elsewhere and do it yourself by systematically turning each classroom into a hub of excellence, one by one, where exemplary practice can be shared.'

Brian looked up, now totally confused, and said to Tom, 'I haven't got a clue what you are talking about.'

The birth of hubs of excellence

Tom sought to add clarity: 'It's such a simple idea, Brian. Start with a member of staff who has significant expertise within any aspect of their work. It doesn't have to be a subject – it can be as simple as promoting a love of reading, thinking skills or drama.'

'What about outdoor learning?' asked Brian.

'Definitely,' said Tom. 'All they do is turn their classroom into an exciting hub which celebrates and promotes a passion for, and excellence within, that area of the school's work.'

Tom spoke and Brian wrote:

The hubs of excellence should be used for:

* Holding three staff workshops over the course of a year.
* Supporting teachers, including newly and recently qualified teachers and those seeking more guidance.

* Taking one short piece of research each year as a source of classroom innovation.
* Creating a library of excellence within that aspect of the school's work and a bank of the best memories built from examples of the most exciting primary practice.

Additionally, the teacher should take a dynamic role in developing review strategies, celebrating good practice and considering next steps with staff and children.

There was a pause before Tom continued to speak and Brian continued to write: 'If you do this rigorously, you will receive something back that will be far greater than payments to recruit and retain teachers.'

Brian looked up and said, 'Tom, that is brilliant.' However, Tom had not yet finished. 'Of course, Brian, this will only be successful if you back it to the hilt.' Brian picked up his pen once more:

Hubs of excellence provide:

* Collaboration, sharing, coaching, modelling and mentoring as commonplace.
* Continuous formal and informal talks about pedagogy.
* A common focus across all hubs.
* A strong sense of efficacy.
* A belief in lifelong learning.
* Teachers and staff who value and celebrate their own learning.

By now the site manager was jingling his keys loudly. It was his subtle way of saying will you please go home?

Give your school the *Teach Primary* factor

Tom said, 'I can hear keys jingling so I've got just one final question: why did you ask about outdoor learning?' Brian explained that he was thinking of promoting the outdoors as a significant way of enhancing pupil learning. Tom agreed that this was a good idea saying, 'The best schools usually have something they are really good at – you recognise it and it grabs you and makes you tingle with excitement as soon as you enter the school.'

Brian told Tom that Andrea had suggested making outdoor learning Springett Lane's unique selling point because all successful businesses should have one. As soon as he said this, Brian sensed that the next butterfly was imminent and reached for his notepad, even though the site manager continued to rattle his keys. He knew this was going to be too important to miss.

> Every school should ask itself this question: can my school contribute an article for *Teach Primary* magazine about an area of exceptional practice that currently exists within the school?
>
> If the answer is no, then what would you want your school to write an article about in three years' time?
>
> Answer: Accelerating pupil progress through high quality outdoor learning.

Making literacy and numeracy beautiful

After a pause and the further jingling of keys, which they ignored, Tom resumed to offer yet another butterfly. He stroked his chin and said, 'There is a further challenge, and this might be the biggest of all. You have to find a way of teaching both literacy and numeracy that provides the children with all the key skills they need, yet celebrates both those subjects as being beautiful. I use the word "beautiful" advisedly. Language in all its forms is beautiful, and when mathematics is taught well it is the most wonderful and beautifully creative subject. If you can achieve that, your school will truly stand out from those who simply follow the government's rhetoric.' Brian noted down:

> Transform teaching and learning in literacy and mathematics so that it celebrates the beautiful creativity that exists within.

And with that butterfly, the notion of beautiful literacy and mathematics was created.

The coasting minister

Things did not seem very beautiful for Rupert Brinton. Tom had rightly identified how government policies were leading to too many teachers leaving the profession. After a series of speeches in which Rupert Brinton criticised the teachers working in 'coasting schools', he was challenged to define what he meant by this term. His response of 'You know what I mean' didn't seem to go down too well with the more serious newspapers because they really didn't know what he meant. Nor apparently did school leaders or inspectors. Parents were especially confused. Grudgingly he said he would define precisely what he meant by the term. A mere forty-five days later, no doubt after many discussions with advisers, a definition was provided on Radio 4's *Today* programme.[3] Many considered it to be muddled as it was predominantly based around those schools that performed below the national average. However, it took no account of the social background of pupils or the circumstances in which the school was operating. Many argued that it was possible for a school in an affluent community to be coasting, whereas a school in an area of disadvantage may not reach the national average but be making huge strides in terms of pupil progress. There was now even more evidence of confusion and mixed messages from political leaders.

A medium term review would have indicated that we had now reached the stage where the prevalent view was that the Department for Education was experiencing a crisis of confidence. It was on a war footing and being run like a sitcom. Its leader was being accused of not providing young people with a rounded education. There were complaints about bullying being rife. Some parents claimed that the secretary of state had a breathtaking arrogance and mixed business with pleasure. It was argued that government policies could lead to a generation of unhealthy children. New evidence pointed to potential bias in the inspection system in order to support specific government initiatives, and now it seemed that their policies were preventing children from receiving an education whereby all their talents could be recognised and developed.

What may have seemed humorous at the start was heading towards crisis point. As things deteriorated further, confusing and mixed messages were adding to the fear and uncertainty.

Many might have wondered if Rupert Brinton really was a suitable person to be secretary of state for education. The prime minister clearly thought he was.

Chapter 11
The problem with fronted adverbial clauses

> Social housing children are told they can only play outside if they keep out of sight of private homes in their cul-de-sac
>
> *Daily Mail* Online, 14 September 2015

You fill up my senses

The evening after Anne Moody's confrontation with Brian, she went home and started to rummage through her wardrobe. She had also been thinking. She would be a very different person when she next spoke to Brian. She was on a mission. Over the years she had become a hoarder. Her wardrobe was not only the place where she stored long lost outfits, but also folders and files and some old notes relating to outdoor education.

About a week later at 10.40 a.m., Brian was walking past Anne Moody's classroom. He glanced up to see if she was there in her beige cardigan talking to a class of children with glazed faces, but she wasn't. In fact, the classroom was empty. 'Good heavens,' Brian thought to himself, 'it must be one of those rare weeks when she actually takes the children to their PE lesson rather than cancel it with some lame excuse.'

Anne Moody was not in her classroom, but she was not doing PE either. Her class was down by the old canal. They had sketchbooks and some were meticulously sketching rusting machinery on the canal side that had not been used for over a century. Other children were carefully focusing on the old warehouse they walked past on their way to and from school. Usually they barely noticed the neglected industrial landscape they were passing but today was different. They were experiencing this area in a deeper way than ever before as they had been asked to complete a sensory trail noting the things they could see, touch, smell and even what they could taste.

As the children closed their eyes, their sense of hearing was heightened and sounds they had never noticed before suddenly became deafening. The rumble of passing traffic on the dual carriageway was constant, a two-carriage train that looked like a relic from the 1970s clattered down the track and a horse whinnied in the distance. The children collaboratively experimented and explored phrases around the powerful words that came into their heads while producing their sketches. They wrote of 'the calmness being corrupted by the repetitively irritating traffic travelling loudly and going boom boom and bang bang across the viaduct'. Others observed the 'busy workmen hunched over piles of dirt, beads of sweat dripping from their foreheads'.[1]

That afternoon they were going to use the activities to create a carefully constructed illustrated story setting. They were going to do it this way because they had been told that this is how many great writers begin. They don't start by sitting behind a desk, because it doesn't work. Our best writers produce descriptions that are so real that the reader believes they can reach out and touch the scene they describe. The sounds are so real, you can almost hear them. Neither do writers start with a study analysing which connectives can be used to create an extended sentence or when to use a fronted adverbial clause to support variation. While these strategies may equip the children to write mechanically at a government-approved age-appropriate level, it is highly probable that great writers don't even know what a fronted adverbial clause actually is.

Before the children had left the classroom, Anne Moody had shown them some writing produced by pupils in the school two decades previously. This had been retrieved from the bottom of her wardrobe. They were intrigued, especially as the parents of children in the class had produced two of the pieces. Anne Moody skilfully used the work to show how the senses had been used to produce sensitive pieces of writing.

As the children left the classroom to make the short walk to the canal, they carried two prompt sheets that would help them to complete the task successfully.

How great writers follow a sensory trail to paint beautiful pictures with words	
	Use exciting vocabulary to describe what you can see.
	Use exciting vocabulary to describe what you can hear.
	Use exciting vocabulary to describe what you can touch.
	Use exciting vocabulary to describe what you can smell.

	Use exciting vocabulary to describe what you can taste.

How great writers paint beautiful pictures with words	
Alliteration	They use sequences of words that begin with the same letter.
Simile	They compare one thing with another using words such as 'like' or 'as'.
Metaphor	They compare one thing with another by saying it is like something else.
Personification	They give an inanimate object human feelings or actions.
Onomatopoeia	They use a word that imitates the sound it represents.
Senses	They use words to describe what they can see, hear, touch, taste and smell.
Nouns and adjectives	A noun is an object, person or place, but great writers use adjectives to add descriptive information to the noun.
Verbs and adverbs	A verb is a word that expresses action. An adverb adds descriptive information to the verb and it normally ends -ly.

Cows hibernate in winter

What had really driven Anne Moody to take her class of children to the canal? This time it had been her turn to be outraged by the newspaper headlines. A survey of how much time children spent outdoors in 2010 indicated that between a quarter and half of all children believed that 'cows hibernate in winter, grey squirrels are native to this country, conkers come from oak (or maybe beech, or is it fir?), and of course there's no such thing as a leaf that can soothe a nettle sting'. The survey argued that it was not really the fault of the youngsters because 64% of the children surveyed played outside less than once a week, 28% of them had not been on a country walk in the last year and 20% had never climbed a tree.[2]

The survey was of 2,000 8- to 12-year-olds for the TV channel Eden and was one of many similar studies. Unsurprisingly, more children could identify a Dalek than an owl. Most play indoors more often than outdoors. The distance our children stray from home on their own has shrunk by 90% since the 1970s. More children are now admitted to British hospitals for injuries incurred falling out of bed than falling out of trees. Today just 43% of adults think it is safe for children to play outdoors unsupervised. This could well be reflected in a survey carried out in May 2016: the Canal and River Trust found that 30% of children couldn't recognise the sound of a duck or a fox. They considered there was now a serious genera-tion gap in children's knowledge of nature and set about creating a mobile phone app which would help youngsters to identify wildlife.[3]

Now, to add further complication to the problem of growing up in the twenty-first century, there were reports of a housing develop-ment in Glastonbury that banned children from playing on bikes, scooters and skateboards near to private housing. The report was in the *Daily Mail* so even Anne Moody thought it best to treat the article with a pinch of salt. But she also knew that many of the adults living around Springett Lane could make harsh judgements about children having a good time outdoors.

By the end of the day, Anne Moody's class had carefully produced their illustrated story settings. Some children had worked in pairs so they could collaboratively explore the richness of the English language. However, she regarded herself as being in a battle to the death with Brian Smith and she was determined to keep up the momentum. That evening she produced a handwritten list of twenty-five outdoor activities she felt the children should be entitled to experience as they passed through Springett Lane Primary School. She was determined to talk Brian through each of them systematically. She even added an extra two just for good measure.

Twenty-five and a bit things children should have the opportunity to do outdoors:

1. Consider creating opportunities to experience the outdoors at night and by moonlight. This could include the use of stories around a fire-pit they have built or a night walk examining how the locality is different in the dark. The children could use torches to go on a mystery tour or a treasure trail using their experiences to contrast night and day. Alternatively, we could work with a local astronomical society which could bring along telescopes for a 'star watch' and examine the majesty of the night skies.

2. As a class, the children should collectively experience the sunrise and sunset from an appropriate nearby location. This could easily be possible in January or February by just extending the school day slightly. We could also couple this with the opportunity to hear the dawn chorus.

3. The school should adopt a footpath. Many local councils run 'adopt a footpath' schemes, whereby an organisation agrees to look after a path. A class of children could do this and walk along it in different seasons of the year, recording the changes using digital photography or sketching. Sketches could be made of wild flowers or the different species of bird life could be recorded and their interactions noted. The children would also ensure that the footpath is kept clear and in a good condition. Alternatively, similar activities could be carried out in a local park.

4. Children should find out how granddad managed without his iPad. Grandparents could talk about what they did when they were children and how they used the outdoors. We should encourage the children to re-live their carefree escapades in the days before risk assessments and

safeguarding by creating a day when they emulate
their grandparents (but we might have to do a risk
assessment first!).

5. Consider feeding mammals during the winter months.
Try tempting hedgehogs with dog food or squirrels/
badgers with nuts. We could consider having a
movement-activated camera focused on the spot during
key times or when the children are not at school.

6. We should take a short trip back to nature. Most people in
Britain live within easy travelling distance of one of the
nation's 1,500 nature reserves. The children could develop
ongoing links with organisations such as the RSPB or
the Wildfowl and Wetlands Trust.

7. Let the children create their own nature trails. Challenge
the pupils to devise their own trail around the school
grounds or local woodlands, devising appropriate publicity
material or guidebooks. As part of this activity, or as a
stand-alone activity, we could challenge the children to
develop their observational skills by playing games such
as 'find ten different creatures' or 'find ten plants'.

8. Be inspired by the 1970s sitcom The Good Life and develop
or rent an allotment where children use appropriately sized
tools to plant and harvest their own fruit and vegetables.
Once quality checks had been made, these could be used
for school meals or sold in the community. The children
could develop their own 'five a day' schemes. Different
year groups could take responsibility for different types of
crops or different parts of the allotment. Produce from the
allotment could help a class to run a restaurant for a day.

9. Keep chickens. We need to check this one out with the local
authority first, but between two and four chickens will keep
an average size family in eggs for a week and children
will love collecting them. It might also be possible to adopt
battery hens and give them a better lifestyle, but we will
need guidance on chicken houses, runs, feeders, etc.

10. Explore the local river. Instead of children studying the
route of a river on an interactive whiteboard indoors, or
simply labelling a worksheet, consider a rich and vivid

project around the story of our local river. Let the children see it as a youthful bubbling spring on the mountainside and encourage them to paddle in the clear waters. Help them to spot fish and wildlife. They could examine how humans have used (and sometimes abused) the river from its source to the sea.

11. Explore prehistoric nature. Many children have a fascination with dinosaurs, and the UK is full of reminders of that prehistoric age. A walk along the right beach will often uncover a wide range of fossils for the children to study.

12. Heighten the senses by encouraging the children to use all their senses at once. Take them on a walk or ask them to sit in a particular habitat and consider what they can see, hear, smell, touch and possibly taste. In a natural environment this could include birdsong and the wind in the trees. However, the approach works just as well in built-up or congested areas, or places that experience different types of pollution. Encourage the use of sketching and descriptive writing. Could the location be used later as a story setting? Could the children produce descriptive writing using an acrostic form, or where the first line begins with A, followed by B, C, D, etc.

13. Reading outdoors can be fun and relaxing. It is an especially brilliant place to read nature books, outdoor adventure books or poetry about the natural world. We could build a special storyteller's chair with seats gathered around it.

14. Introduce flora and fauna to the grounds so the children can learn to experience a wide variety of wildlife through activities such as making birdbaths and feeders, growing native plants and observing what happens through the seasons.

15. Examine hidden environments by placing a flat piece of board face down on the ground and leaving it for a few days. It doesn't need to be large. Then, when the children return a few days later and observe how many creatures have taken shelter there, they can try to identify them and

find out more about them. It's a process that you can keep repeating every month.

16. Observe the process from frogspawn to tadpoles to baby frogs by collecting spawn in the spring and watching it develop. By filling a tank with rainwater and adding some plants, the tadpoles can feed on algae. As time moves on, feed the growing tadpoles on boiled lettuce, fish food or chopped up meat. Add some stones so the froglets can climb out of the water. When the time is right, release them back where you originally found the spawn.

17. Consider developing survival activities by asking the children to build a shelter or den. How waterproof can they make it? Can they design it so that it retains an element of heat and is strong enough to withstand the wind or being pushed over? Could the children camp out on the school field or elsewhere overnight, carefully planning the steps they would need to take?

18. Build a weather station and get the children to build up their own database on the weather conditions in the school grounds. Consider sharing the outcomes with schools elsewhere in the UK or the world. Also explore the micro-climates that may exist around the school, finding out if there are any areas which seem warmer because they trap more sun or colder due to the amount of shade.

19. Try wildlife (or other) photography. Cameras could be regularly taken on outings. Alternatively, they could be set up on a tripod facing a bird table and triggered automatically to capture images of the different species that visit. Photography can also be used in the built environment. Images could be incorporated into the children's writing or presentations. The children could even make their own documentary films. At the end of the school year, the children could have their own 'Oscars' evening screening the best films and visual images.

20. Regularly take good quality sketchbooks out and encourage the children to sit quietly and capture their observations. However, make sure you teach drawing techniques and allow enough time for children to produce

work they can be proud of and that reflects perseverance and genuine quality. The sketchbooks could stay with each child as they pass through the school so they have a record of progression, prompting them always to make sure the drawing they are working on is better than previous ones.

21. Create a school pond. Many schools have created ponds within the school grounds that attract a variety of aquatic and bird life. The children can pond dip at appropriate times of the year and build up their own nature journals.

22. Collect rock samples or go under the ground in order to introduce the children to the world of geology. This could involve a visit to a show cave. We could also get the children to collect different kinds of rock – hard or soft rocks, different colours or ones that shine or contain minerals.

23. Get wet or go wild with canoeing or sailing or other outdoor activities that bring an element of adventure into the lives of children. (The Primary National Strategy produced a superb video called 'Earthwatch' which demonstrated the impact of this work.[4])

24. Cuddle up to creepy-crawlies by challenging the children to catch as many insects or spiders as they can (taking care to avoid wasps, bees, hornets and red ants). Using insect catchers that are available from most large suppliers, the children can use magnifying glasses to identify the distinguishing features.

25. Make the most of pedal-power when children have cycle-to-school days or, alternatively, set up a cycle tour that might stop off at places of natural or man-made interest. The rangers at the local country park may be able to help, especially if they hire out cycles.

26. We should challenge those who make the laws if we think there are unfair restrictions on where children can play or take part in certain activities. The children should suggest ways of making that activity safe and convince people that changes would be a good thing.

27. Adopt the sunny day rule. When the weather is just right, being inside feels so wrong; therefore, why not simply go

outside for a story, to play some physical mathematics games, etc. Wouldn't it be wonderful if all our classrooms had patio doors that opened out onto an external learning space, after which we could build our own outdoor classroom ...

Children live in a toxic climate of porn, bullying and failure

Meanwhile, there was even more evidence that Rupert Brinton was out of touch with reality. Not only were children growing up in a world where they didn't explore their natural environments, but the charity Young Minds had also produced evidence that the nation was living on a mental health time bomb. Their report indicated that young people were experiencing an onslaught of stress, bullying and sexual pressure at school. The campaign director attacked government ministers for their role in adding to this pressure and accused the Department for Education of being obsessed with testing and academic success rather than the well-being of children. The World Health Organization estimates that by 2030 depression will be the biggest health problem in the western world, therefore well-being should be a key part of the curriculum.[5]

But the secretary of state was now about to add to the problem by replacing coursework with a far more stressful regime of testing at GCSE level. In November 2013, *The Guardian* accused him of removing any second chances for students and of an over-reliance on 'an O-level style eggs-in-one-basket summer examination', the like of which had been abandoned over a quarter of a century earlier.[6]

Chapter 12
This is the kind of English up with which I will not put

Literacy in our schools at 'Dickensian-era levels' warns minister as classics are ignored

Daily Mail Online, 8 February 2012

There is an error in the sentence below. Write the correction in the box.

The confused cyclist weren't sure where to go.

Brian read the question twice, not because he didn't know the answer – it was through a sense of despair. It was a question from Rupert Brinton's new spelling and grammar test.[1] To Brian it represented everything that was wrong in his own education. Rightly or wrongly, he thought it was a test written for 'posh' kids. He read it a third time to confirm just how bad it was and then tossed it to one side saying to himself, 'Who cares, it's just a miserable sentence that isn't worth correcting anyway.' One of his Year 6 children had earlier written in response: 'The confused cyclist weren't any better at Inglish neither.'

Somehow that response reflected the magic of the English language better than the answer deemed to be correct by the Standards and Testing Agency. Brian started reflecting on his earlier conversation with Tom on the teaching of literacy. So much time had passed since the advent of the literacy strategy in 1998. There are many who believe that our nation has a rich, vivid and beautiful language, but it was now deemed acceptable to put a puerile sentence in front of children and ask them to correct it, when it wasn't really worth the effort. Brian had read Rupert Brinton's new guidance on how to assess children's writing at Key Stage 2 and quickly realised that it had taken the most wonderful and creative language in the world and potentially turned it into little more than a series of tests and exercises which could be marked right or wrong. From his own education, he knew that Shakespeare melted language into a kind of cauldron, conjuring magical transformations. Adjectives became verbs and often adverbs became nouns, such as when Prospero talks about the 'dark backward' of time. This wasn't 'correct' in any era, but such free magic was probably more likely to occur when correct usage meant what sounded best, rather than adherence to the rules.

Brian understood that he came from a different era. He could write well and there were occasions when his children's stories had been published. He knew the key aspects of punctuation. He recognised the importance of grammar but he was not a 'grammar snob'. The nation had far too many of those people. At his own primary school, a Catholic nun called Sister Agnes had whacked him around the ears regularly with a table tennis bat, which she kept in her habit for that purpose, for using the phrase 'different to' rather than 'different from'. It took him a further twenty-seven years to find out that both are deemed to be perfectly acceptable by the Oxford English Dictionary. Brian reconsidered the term 'grammar snob' and wondered if this was a phrase he had invented. He googled the term to see whether he could claim originality. He found himself intrigued by the responses. It seemed that too often grammar is associated with social etiquette and many people had experienced being told off when they appeared to get things wrong. Brian already knew that grammar did not relate to pronunciation or the meaning of words because that was about dialect and vocabulary. Grammar was simply about the way a language organises words, putting them in order and showing their relationship to each other. Brian started to write:

> A significant problem has been telling people just how mistaken and rubbish their language is. But with precisely zero foundation. Actually, we are not mistaken or wrong in any aspect of our language and we are all language experts – no, beyond experts; we are geniuses – at English grammar. Unless you are suffering from severe neural damage or you are drunk or drugged enough to make walking in a straight line quite a task, you, as a native speaker of English, do not make mistakes when you speak.[2]

So there it was. The children at Springett Lane Primary School, who were mostly native speakers of English, were also experts at language. He refused to accept that they were geniuses at language or grammar because that sounded arrogant, but being positive about their language seemed to be a really good starting point, especially when too often we speak of children in deprived communities entering school with a language deficit. Brian had been so impressed by the extract that he made a note to order a copy of Harry Ritchie's book *English for Natives*.

Brian reconsidered those stern and scary grammarians. He now regarded such people as dangerous because of the perverse pleasure they seemed to get from correcting or deriding the language of others, inferring that they had received some kind of superior education. This was dangerous for the kids at Springett Lane Primary School who needed encouragement to use language with enjoyment rather than experience correction or ridicule.

Indeed, Brian himself was unsure about many grammatical terms and wasn't sure if a greater knowledge of the pluperfect progressive would make him a better writer or not. Brian entered the teaching profession just after the publication of *A Language for Life*, better known as the Bullock Report. It remains the last major independent survey of the teaching of English in our schools. The report criticised the use of bland grammar exercises about lost and confused cyclists, pointing out that they did absolutely nothing to improve the quality of children's writing.[3]

The newspapers had recently published reports based on an article in *The Idler* magazine which listed contenders for its 'Bad Grammar' awards. One of the award winners was a letter by a group of academics about the national curriculum, which included the line: 'Much of it demands too much too young.'[4]

The sentence was given a top ten place in the Bad Grammar awards because it confused an adjective with an adverb. Meanwhile, another group of grammarians analysed the sentence closely and deemed the sentence to be perfectly acceptable because many words function as both an adjective and an adverb. Hours were spent as the debate vehemently raged, or maybe the debate raged vehemently? Who knows and who cares. Anybody reading the sentence about the national curriculum knew precisely what it meant. Brian fervently believed that the national curriculum *did* demand too much of our young people. He also knew that grammar should be seen as a convention to support writing and make it richer, rather than a set of imposed edicts. He was reminded of a long lost quote from George Bernard Shaw. He wrote it down as he knew he would want to use it at some stage in the future:

There is a busybody on your staff who devotes a lot of his time to chasing split infinitives. Every good literary craftsman splits his infinitives when the sense demands it. I call for the immediate dismissal of this pedant. It is of no consequence whether he decides to go quickly, or quickly to go or to quickly go. The important thing is that he should go at once.[5]

Brian also thought it captured a beautiful and creative use of language.

Many within education considered that the introduction of the spelling and grammar test was another sham in which Rupert Brinton had ridden roughshod over his advisers in some kind of extraordinary conjuring trick. In April 2011, Lord Bew produced an interim report into assessment and accountability. By the time the final report came out two months later, an appendix had suddenly appeared with a crash like an unforeseen meteor from another planet, saying there should be a Key Stage 2 spelling and grammar test.[6]

Brian turned his attention to the newspaper, glancing at the *Daily Mail* headline, but then his iPad pinged, indicating an email had arrived. It was Eve. The message simply read:

Hi Bri,

Just to let you know I have been thinking about you. I miss your company. How are things at Springett Lane? I see that politician dude is still looking backwards to the nineteenth century rather than forwards into the 2020s. I see he wants to reintroduce the writing of lines for wayward children who switch off or misbehave during dull lessons. That won't do much to develop a love of writing, Brian, or even save the rainforest from deforestation when paper is used for such mundane purposes.[7]

Don't let them grind you down. Leave your grey and cloudy island behind and join me in the sun. In fact, please write 100 times, 'Eve is fabulous. I should go and live with her in California.'

Eve x

Could a handful of guinea pig wee provide a solution?

As ever it was as though Eve had read his mind. The story certainly indicated that once again the secretary of state was intent on looking backwards, especially when it came to the teaching of English. It seemed poignant. Earlier that day he had been in Miss Jones' Year 3 classroom observing a literacy lesson. The previous day the children had been to a local tourist attraction, Pets Corner. They had clearly had a fabulous time. On the way in, Brian welcomed all the children (as he always did) and they were still buzzing with the excitement of the visit. They rushed up to Brian saying, 'Mr Smith, Mr Smith, you will never guess what we did yesterday …' And all the details came out in a garbled rush, with the children interrupting each other as they each made a bid to tell their part of the story about the animals they had encountered. But by 9.15 a.m. the experience had been killed stone dead.

Until this point, Brian had held the work of Keely Jones in some regard. Sometimes he wished he had invested more time in talking to her. She was in her fifth year of teaching, yet somehow he felt that he didn't really know what made her tick. However, her lessons were always planned meticulously and, after very careful consideration, he had made her the literacy subject leader. She had a really good working knowledge of the framework and assessment structures and used the guidance and sample lesson plans available on the internet very effectively.

During a lesson observation on the day after the visit to Pets Corner, he revised his opinion and realised that perhaps the frameworks had led to a culture of over-planning and micromanagement. In the lesson, the children had been asked to write an account of the visit the previous day using time connectives because that was what the literacy framework required them to do. Brian was certainly pleased that they were using the visit as a stimulus and guessed that it must be important the children knew what time connectives were, although he wasn't fully convinced that this couldn't just happen naturally. But he was most disappointed with what happened next. The direct teaching was good and, it has to be said, the children knew exactly what a time connective was and precisely when to use one, but the children produced writing that was dull and unimaginative, and some of it wasn't even as interesting as that! The children wrote about getting on the bus, when they ate their sandwiches and at what point they visited the shop, but no child managed to capture the magic of the fabulous experience that had excited them the day before.

Now, we know that Brian was passionate about the English language. He believed it to be wonderfully rich and that well-chosen words could be used to paint stunning pictures that could potentially transport you on a magic carpet to a different place and time. However, today there was no sign of either carefully chosen words or stunning pictures. The children seemed to be locked into a boring and forgettable academic task. In a well-constructed lesson, the children could have been transported back to their thrilling experience, but instead they were seated at their desks undertaking an exercise that represented a much lower level of challenge. It was an academic exercise that simply encouraged teachers to tick a box relating to a nationally prescribed framework.

Brian looked at his watch. This was one of those lesson observations that dragged on. It was starting to feel like the seasons were changing outside, or maybe it was like the music of Wagner because it had wonderful moments and tedious half hours. Brian suddenly became conscious of how long he had been staring at his feet and pulled himself together.

He knew he had to offer feedback on a lesson that he really hadn't enjoyed. In desperation, he went to speak to Simon who was working at a nearby table. He may only have been 7 years old but Brian knew he always had a good tale to tell. Brian read over Simon's work then intuitively asked him which bit of the previous day had been the best. Simon's response came quick as a flash: 'It was when I got to hold a guinea pig. The first thing I knew was that the fur was so soft and warm and then I could feel its little heart beating against the palm of my hand. Next, its sharp claws were scratching at my fingers as it tried to wriggle and get free and so I grasped it even harder. As I did, the guinea pig did a wee on my hands and they went all hot and sticky. This made me feel as though I would drop it but I didn't. I just tightened my hands around its soft body and wondered what to do with the guinea pig wee.'

Brian sat there silently as though his hands were metaphorically filling with guinea pig urine and he had nowhere to put it. The reality was he was deep in thought. A solution was starting to materialise.

The conversation with Simon was a pivotal moment in Brian's thinking. However, the conversation with Keely during the feedback was to prove even more defining. In a bid to be positive he had suggested to Miss Jones that if she had asked the children to describe the best bit of the day using time connectives, the quality of writing and language may have been richer. Miss Jones had lowered her spectacles at this point and looked Brian full in the face as though he was a complete idiot, and said, 'But Year 3 don't cover adventurous vocabulary until after February half term.' Brian gasped in despair. He thought of the sensitivity of feeling in the writing in Anne Moody's class the day before and realised there were better ways of doing things if he was to create truly beautiful English lessons at Springett Lane.

Brian had left the feedback meeting in consternation and looked through the work schemes that were being followed. He then took a relatively unsystematic trawl through some of the children's exercise books, and his immediate reaction was that the school was placing far too strong an emphasis on the technical and grammatical features of writing while paying very little attention to how a great writer creates magic with words. He also recognised that it was highly unlikely that the children in his school would currently be able to do this, even if they did know what a connective was and how to define an expanded noun phrase.

Once more, Brian cast his mind back to the Bullock Report and reached for it from his shelf. This was the first time the book had been opened in a decade, which was a shame because it is filled with gems. He started to write:

> What has been shown is that the teaching of traditional analytical grammar does not appear to improve performance in writing … What is questionable is the practice of setting of exercises for the whole class, irrespective of need, and assuming that this will improve every pupil's ability to handle English.[8]

Brian was now despondent because, forty-two years on, tests were being devised based on this discredited principle. Brief glimpses at the catalogues of educational publishers indicated they were already preparing to line the pockets of their directors and shareholders by publishing mundane exercises for classes of children to complete in preparation for Rupert Brinton's spelling and grammar tests.

Brian flipped open his laptop and idly typed in, 'What kind of English teaching is right for our pupils?' He started to read, and the frightening thing was that it was like reading the *Daily Mail* headline all over again, but this had been written almost a hundred years earlier. It seems that even then people were looking back over their shoulders, believing that there had been some golden age of education. In the Newbolt Report of 1921, the Departmental Committee of the Board of Education reported:

> Messrs Vickers Ltd find 'great difficulty in obtaining junior clerks who can speak and write English clearly and correctly, especially those aged from 15 to 16 years'. Messrs Lever Bros Ltd say 'it is a great surprise and disappointment to us to find that our young employees are so hopelessly deficient in their command of English'. The Boots Pure Drug Co. say:

'Teaching of English in present day schools produces very little command of the English language … Our candidates do not appreciate the value of shades of meaning, and while able to do imaginative composition, show weakness in work which requires accurate description or careful arrangement of detail.'[9]

The strange thing about these comments is that they come from an era of high accountability and payment by results. Schools would have been punished financially if they failed to meet the requirements placed upon them, such as teaching illative coordination (in which the second of two principal sentences is placed in logical conclusion or inference with the first, and that the conjunctions which join them are therefore, wherefore and consequently). An emphasis was also placed on schools to teach the copulative conjunction (and the definition of a copulative conjunction really is best left to the imagination). What was clear to Brian was that there never had been a golden age for the teaching of grammar, but maybe there had always been grammar snobs who had caused damage!

A smile spread across his face. He thought of the field he drove past every weekend. The farmer who sought to sell his produce at the roadside had a sign. It was only a piece of hardboard nailed to a simple wooden stake and the writing was in a kind of whitewash. It simply said 'POTATOES' in bold capital letters. It had stood there for many a year, and there was very little evidence of people stopping to make a purchase. Late one evening, a local wag had taken a paintbrush and his own whitewash and added to the sign so that it now said:

POTATOES
TWINNED WITH POMMES DE TERRE

This had made Brian laugh out loud and also, no doubt, done wonders for trade. He loved the ingenuity of words and how they worked together. In an attempt to lift his depression he started to search the internet once more.

Brian quickly found numerous lists of the nation's favourite words. One suggested serendipity was the most loved word, while another promoted quidditch, the fictional game played by witches and wizards, and surely whimsical was a marvelous word to describe this mythical pastime. Brian also discovered that a poodle-faker was a man who spent too much time drinking tea with upper class ladies and a scrimshanker is a person who avoids or takes no responsibility for their work. He discovered that if you should ever encounter somebody who is a quarrelsome shrew of a woman you could legitimately describe her as a termagant, but by contrast a flighty young woman who is prone to showing off could officially be referred to as frippet. Brian found people who liked crunchy words such as brittle, crackly, crusty and splintering. There seemed to be a suggestion that more mature, academic individuals would prefer to turn their words into some form of elaborate peregrination by mansplaining and using elegant and flowery words. However, by contrast, he also knew that the children at Springett Lane preferred giggly-sniggly words such as gurgle, bottom and burp. One internet contribution was from a person who always burst into uncontrolled laughter at the word shrubbery.

Brian now had a real dilemma. He knew he wanted every lesson to become a language rich one and for the children to engage with the power of words in their writing. He knew that one of the key purposes of writing is to bring into this world something that is both wonderful and unique, and that he wanted this to happen for the children at Springett Lane on a termly basis. He had also become aware that Anne Moody and her beige cardigan, who had been his scourge for so many years, may be better equipped to achieve this than the younger Keely Jones, who seemed to have a deep understanding of national frameworks and grammatical structures but was less capable of eliciting an inspirational response from the children. He knew it might require a radical rethink. He was aware that he might need to pay Tom a visit, but in the meantime, it was nearly time to meet Andrea. He put on his coat and set off for the wine bar.

Dumped between two presidents (and by Andrea)

During the first glass of wine, Brian explained his dilemma. During the second, Andrea reached for the notepad, drew a series of concentric circles and explained the root of his dilemma:[11]

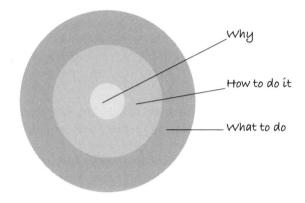

Brian looked at the diagram intrigued as Andrea started to explain: 'Most people are proficient at their jobs but not necessarily great leaders of an organisation, and these people start powerfully on the outside of the concentric circles. In short, they know what they have to do when they get to work. Some move to the second ring because they know how to do it well. However, very few of them know why they do it, or why they do it in a particular way, and therefore never get to the central ring.'

There was a pause before she continued: 'For truly great leaders, though, the process works in reverse. They fully understand the purpose of their job and why it must be done in a particular way. However, sometimes they are less clear on how to do it or what to do. They have a vision for the future but often need to empower others to get the right jobs done in the right way. When Nelson Mandela was freed from prison and became president of South Africa, he had a deeply held belief that a new nation could be built on a policy of peace and reconciliation. He didn't necessarily know how it should be done because that was an activity for the policy-makers and others. In the early 1960s, President Kennedy told American citizens that the United States would put a man on the moon by the end of the decade. He knew why he wanted to do it. It was because he wanted to demonstrate to the world that the

Americans were world leaders in research and development in the space age. However, he had no idea what to do or how to do it. He regarded that as other people's domain.'

Andrea continued with her analysis: 'Keely sits on the outside of the circles because, clearly, she knows what is required of her currently, but she has never questioned why she does it that way. If you want to change her practice, and others', you have to explain the "why" of the changes first so that she and others feel empowered to follow. And when you achieve that, then you will be on the verge of becoming a great leader.'

Brian was unnerved. His work felt insignificant beside those who had worked to bring peace and reconciliation to South Africa or land a man on the moon.

Andrea was looking superb that evening and the wine was relaxing, so it came as a blow when she stood up and said she had to leave because she had an early start the following morning. In reality, Andrea was leaving early because she wanted the conversation to remain friendly and professional. She really enjoyed Brian's company, but she knew she didn't want any emotional entanglement getting in the way of their project. Brian suddenly felt lonely. He had really looked forward to Andrea's company and now she was gone. He ordered another glass of wine, then forced himself back to the task of thinking about literacy.

Great English teachers make the world go round

Brian now knew three things. First, he wanted the children to have high levels of confidence in using both written and spoken language. This was one of the key routes to them becoming confident and aspirational individuals. And he wanted them to be able to possess this in a variety of situations, whether it be in front of an audience, in an interview or simply in casual conversation. Second, he wanted the children to be able to paint pictures with words, as a great writer would do. Each term he wanted each child to create significant and beautiful pieces of writing that were so powerful they would potentially withstand the course of time. Third, he wanted the children to be totally absorbed in high quality children's literature.

Once more he reached for his notepad to record his thoughts. The words in the boxes came first and the title came second. Brian noted his pleasure in creating a six word story as a heading.

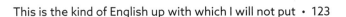

Mastering words that can paint pictures		
Children must be able to speak with confidence in the right way and at the right time so that the listener has absolute clarity, and in a way that has the capacity to paint pictures in the mind.	Children must be able to write with confidence in the right way and at the right time so that the reader has absolute clarity, some of which will have the capacity to paint pictures in the mind.	Children must become absorbed in high quality children's literature and the kind of stories that paint pictures in the mind.

Brian wondered what butterflies Tom would have to offer and reached for his mobile phone to make contact. But the evening was suddenly about to become more complicated as the doors of the wine bar opened and in walked a very smartly dressed Anne Moody.

Brian tried to sink lower into his seat and thought about how he could exit before he was spotted. This was a wasted exercise because he had already been seen. Anne Moody was also thinking about her exit route because she didn't want to be spotted by her boss either, on this night of all nights. She cursed Match.com under her breath, fearing that the date she had set up would simply become the big joke at next week's senior leadership meeting.

A syllabus for the 1940s

Around the corner there was even more negative press for Rupert Brinton as his views on literacy had come under further fire after the secretary of state had instructed examination boards to drop texts such as Arthur Miller's *The Crucible*, John Steinbeck's *Of Mice and Men* and Harper Lee's Pulitzer Prize-winning *To Kill a Mockingbird* because he didn't like them. The criticism was harsh and to the point. *The Guardian* quoted a senior lecturer at King's College London who claimed that Rupert Brinton's curriculum was out of the 1940s, tedious and would grind children down. The same article included the question, 'Since when was the wretched [Brinton] allowed to dictate what children read. This man is a dangerous philistine.'[12]

Research had already shown that a child's capacity to enjoy a good book considerably enhances their life chances.[13] This was reflected in the huge number of educationalists and academics who rushed to comment and who recognised that the texts Rupert Brinton was so keen to disparage had the capacity to have a profound and positive effect on young people's lives.

Chapter 13

Three-generational lessons within a fourth-generation curriculum

> Latin lessons for state school pupils aged five in language revival
>
> *Daily Mail* Online, 1 December 2010

The evening was to become even more complicated because, just after Anne Moody had taken the first sip of the large glass of red wine, which she hoped would help her cope with whatever was going to happen next, her mobile phone vibrated with a text message to say that her potential suitor from the dating site was not going to turn up. Her immediate reaction was one of relief because next week's gossip had been avoided. But she then found herself saying 'Damn, damn, damn' under her breath as she was still trapped in a wine bar with a large glass of Merlot, not knowing how to escape. Worse than that, her boss was staring at her.

Brian Smith was indeed staring. In fact, he thought it would have been very rude not to because she had obviously put a great deal of care into her appearance that evening. There was no sign of the beige cardigan tonight. Anne Moody intuitively turned to see if she was still being watched, and as she did so their eyes met.

After an uncomfortable few seconds, which seemed much longer, Brian decided to do the chivalrous thing and wander over to ask if she would like to join him. He considered this to be a safe option because he figured that Anne Moody was bound to be in the bar because she was meeting someone and would therefore decline. However, when he asked the question, Anne Moody decided there was no use pretending that she was waiting for someone who was not going to turn up. Feeling trapped, she agreed and they both walked across to Brian's table. Possibly out of fear, or possibly nerves, Anne Moody started to take ever bigger swigs of wine, and soon her brain and her mouth were working slightly out of synchronisation. Before long, she was telling him the story of how she had been stood up and how desperate she was to find a soulmate with whom to share her life. She begged Brian not to ridicule her to their colleagues, especially as she was trying really hard to implement his ideas because she really wanted to earn his respect.

As many people might, Brian felt uncomfortable with Anne's outpourings and seemed to find his wine glass fascinating during this part of the conversation. However, he did take the opportunity to steer the subject to a more comfortable area when she mentioned school. While he did this, Anne Moody was drinking faster and faster in an attempt to calm her nerves.

Brian knew that he needed to take the tension out of the situation by suggesting that she relax, while reassuring her that anything that was said outside of school hours had nothing to do with anybody else. After a brief silence, he turned the subject back to school and the quality of the children's writing. In order to bolster Anne Moody's fragile self-confidence he said, 'I have been thinking about the list you produced relating to the types of rich learning activities the children should experience outdoors – it is really powerful. I wonder if each child could have some form of a passport and we stamp it each time they successfully complete a learning challenge? We could even send it home with the end-of-year report.'

The wine was now having an effect on Anne Moody and this may have helped her to feel bold. She considered her response thoughtfully and said, 'It could be a helpful strategy in driving a school focus on outdoor learning, and the children might love it too, but the main thing is that teachers should just use the outdoors intuitively because it is the right thing to do. It would be sad if teachers used the natural world simply because they needed to complete a checklist. There has to be a balance, and the messages must be given to the staff very carefully.'

This time it was Brian's turn to become pensive. He felt he had been accused of producing a simplistic tick list that could get in the way of the kind of deep learning the children had experienced by the old canal, and so he said, 'I was impressed by the quality of the children's writing following your class visit to the canal.' Then, remembering his earlier conversation with Tom, he asked what was to become a golden question when he enquired, 'How did you feel at the end of the lesson, and how did you think the children felt?'

Her response was quick and a little surprising: 'I felt really pleased with the beautiful, rich language they had used and, when I got home, it seemed like this was the best school day I had enjoyed in a long time. As for the children, they felt like real writers – writing for a real purpose – rather than undertaking an academic exercise between a mathematics lesson and a visit to the IT suite. I think the visual impetus is important to the children; it helps to make the lesson memorable. When I trained as a teacher they told me that, every now and then, we should try to teach a lesson that is so good that the children can't wait to get home and tell their parents all about it.'

Brian was pleased to note that Anne Moody used the word 'beautiful' to describe the rich language used by the children. His mind was racing as he recalled his conversation with Tom when they had spoken of those three-generational lessons that had the potential to remain in children's lives forever. With the help of Anne Moody, he now realised that one of the key elements to preparing three-generational lessons was to plan for not only how the children would feel at the end of the lesson but also how the teacher would feel. The ideas were rapidly forming in his mind, ideas that could bring an exciting new future for both the teachers at Springett Lane and those young learners who make up Generation Z. Brian had already noted the changes in Anne Moody, and if this approach could transform her then it could transform anybody – while raising two proverbial fingers to the Right Honourable Rupert Brinton. Brian needed Anne Moody to go home now as he had some very serious thinking to do.

At exactly that same moment Andrea had arrived back at her hotel. As she walked up the steps towards reception she started to feel lonely, wishing she was still with Brian, and on an impulse went back to see if he was still there. Ten minutes later she pushed open the doors of the wine bar and immediately saw another woman sitting where she had been just twenty minutes earlier. Andrea was unsure what to do next. Feeling sad and confused, she decided it was best to leave.

Some thirty minutes later, Brian told Anne Moody he must leave as there were things he must do for the following morning. He had been totally unaware of Andrea's brief entrance and exit from the wine bar.

The birth of the three-generational lesson – part 1

Almost nothing needs to be said when you have eyes.

Tarjei Vesaas

Brian was telling the truth when he said he still had work to do. His mind was truly racing. After he got home he reached for his notepad because he was about to invent a totally new format for planning a three-generational lesson. It was going to be free of declared learning objectives and based much more around taking the children on an exciting and memorable mystery tour that would remain with them forever. He knew that not every lesson could be like this, but he also knew that maybe, every now and again, every teacher should produce one lesson that was good enough to last for three generations. Even stranger, the framework that Brian was working on had come straight from the lips of Anne Moody, who he had not respected for very long.

Brian knew that a key element of the three-generational lesson had to be visual. Anne Moody had been right to take the children to the desolate environment around the canal to trigger a response because as much as 40% of everything we learn comes from visual imagery. It helps us to recapture previous learning. Brian started to write:

Generating images within the three-generational lesson (part 1):

*   Visualise the learning environment (which might be the classroom or elsewhere). How will it be laid out, and

what will it look like before the children arrive to create maximum impact?

* Now consider what the resources will look like as they are introduced to the class.
* Try to visualise the children's expressions you are seeking to achieve. Will they be wide eyed or even have their mouths slightly open in excitement and anticipation?
* Try to consider your own location in the room. Where will you stand? When will you lower your body and when will you stand tall? How will you use actions and gestures to make your message stronger?
* Think about how you would like the children to present their work in a high quality way.
* Finally, if appropriate, what clothes should you wear to achieve the right impact?

Brian was pleased with his initial thoughts about planning the three-generational lesson. He could remember reading a book entitled *Talk Like TED*, which analysed the attributes of some of the world's most inspirational speakers who had secured huge audiences for their eighteen-minute online lectures.[1] The book had described how fabulous teachers and speakers use their body to work a room so that it fills with electricity. It argued that the great communicators do not stay in one spot or remain motionless because standing still makes you look rigid, boring and disengaged. They also have animated body movements because they know that gestures can make a strong argument even stronger. This, in turn, provides a sense of 'command presence' – a military term – which makes others want to follow you. Brian reached for the pen once more and wrote:

Thoughts about a teacher's physical location:
Our bodies change our minds.
Our minds can change our behaviour.
Our behaviour can change our outcomes.
Your strength as a teacher comes from within.

Brian thought back to his schooldays when some of his own teachers seemed constantly to be fidgeting, tapping or jingling coins in their pockets and how he had switched off as a result of these irritating habits. He wondered if he dared use video cameras to help teachers identify their annoying habits in order to eradicate them, but he really fancied trying out the idea.

The birth of the three-generational lesson – part 2

> Without knowing the force of words, it is impossible to
> know men.
>
> Confucius

Having thought about how a lesson should unfold visually, Brian now turned his attention to the second key element, that of verbalisation and how the spoken word can bring language to life. A recent headline from the *Daily Mail* had suggested it was time to return to the era when Latin was taught in schools. It conjured up pictures of ancient wooden desks in rows, gowned teachers patrolling the aisles and timid students chanting conjugated verbs. While Rupert Brinton may have applauded such a scene, it sent a chill down Brian's spine. He wanted something very different for the children on the estate around Springett Lane. Brian thought back to what he had read about the nation's most loved words. He wanted his teachers to demonstrate day by day that they had a love of words as they spoke to their classes. He reflected on what he had learned from the book, *Talk Like TED*. As a result, he knew that the second key element of a three-generational lesson was the way in which teachers used language, and he knew there were three elements to the successful use of language.

First, it is through language that great teachers demonstrate their passion, and when this is unleashed it engages the learners around them. Second, he wanted his teachers to master the art of storytelling because stories provide facts and knowledge with soul. Research has shown that the brain becomes active when listening to stories. Andrew Stanton, the writer of *Toy Story*, once said, 'We all love stories; we were born for them.'[2] Brian recalled Eve's email about the French national curriculum, which placed an increased emphasis on children learning how to live good lives and distinguishing vice from virtue, justice from injustice. He knew that if this was to be achieved, stories had a significant role to play. It is stories that plant ideas and emotions in the brain. Brian also knew that some of the best stories could be personal or, if they involved others, they might be about heroes and villains, good overcoming evil or turning adversity into success. When this is done well, the teacher will be leading a performance in which the art and the science of pedagogy work together hand in hand. Third, Brian knew that, sometimes, great lessons are more like a conversation in which a charismatic teacher skilfully ensures everybody is involved rather than delivers a formal presentation. Also, we all know that some of the best conversations have an element of the unexpected, and if that means the teacher comes in dressed as Henry VIII, then so be it. Brian started to write.

Generating the language within the three-generational lesson (part 2):

* Think about how you will use language to bring the lesson to life. When we teach the children to write, we tell them about alliteration, similes, metaphors and onomatopoeia, but do we demonstrate these as we speak?

* Think about the power of telling short stories (preferably those the teacher has made up from personal experience) that can enhance the learning.

* Think about raising or lowering your voice for effect, and even the power of a short spell of silence, because this can give your words greater impact. Think about the rate at which you speak and also the pitch of your voice to create high and low inflections.

* Think about 'Friends, Romans, countrymen, lend me your ears' and the power of the 'rule of three', because it makes your message clear and memorable. Trios, triads and triplets abound in western culture and that is the truth, the whole truth and nothing but the truth.

* Consider some of the key skills of charisma by thinking about how you use your sparkly eyes to

make contact with a child and then ask a question using well-thought-out words. Then listen to their response and slightly rephrase it to move the lesson on, leading the child to believe they have contributed to a significant part of the lesson.

The birth of the three-generational lesson – part 3

Our feelings are our most genuine paths to knowledge.

Audre Lorde

So far so good! However, Brian knew there was still even more to planning the three-generational lesson. During the ill-fated meeting in the wine bar, Anne Moody had told Brian that, after her successful outdoor lesson by the canal, she had realised that the children had felt like real writers and she had wanted to go home and celebrate. That took Brian into the missing third element of his three-generational lesson, and it related to feelings. Brian checked back through his notebook and found this earlier entry:

The importance of feelings in education:
What if we were to plan for how children feel at the end of a lesson, especially if it leaves them with a heightened sense of empathy or anger about injustice, or with a desire to change the world for the better?

Brian now knew that if teachers could create the right emotional hooks to stimulate Generation Z with a desire to make a positive difference, it would release the dopamine in the brain that stimulates great learning. By focusing on projects that teach right from wrong, good from evil, fair from unfair and what makes our world beautiful or ugly, the children would start to respect the increasing fragility of humanity and the planet. If this were to be replicated across the country, then maybe Generation Z would indeed solve significant problems for the world. It could stimulate genuine action around global warming. We could learn how to support a population of seven billion plus. People from all faiths and cultures would finally learn how to live harmoniously in rapidly changing communities. Brian wrote:

Generating feelings within the three-generational lesson
(part 3):

Teachers should sometimes target the heart first and
the brain second, and think about how they want children
to feel at the end of a lesson. For example:

* If children are learning about trench warfare in the
  First World War, then there is nothing wrong with
  them feeling sad.
* If children are studying recycling then maybe they
  should feel that they can make a difference.
* If children have been studying sweatshop labour in
  developing countries, then there is nothing wrong
  with them feeling angry about the exploitation of
  vulnerable people.
* There is nothing wrong with the teacher planning how
  they want to feel at the end of a lesson and having the
  sense of a job well done.

The clock was approaching midnight. Brian was pleased with his
night's work. Just before he turned in, he made a rash decision. He
had really missed Andrea when she left the wine bar and now he
felt very lonely. He decided he would invite her to go away with him
for the weekend. While he feared rejection, he also considered that
regretting a lost opportunity would be even worse. He knew Andrea
turned off her phone at night, so he decided to send a message there
and then because he may not be feeling so bold in the morning.

Our deepest fear is that of not measuring up

Tullian Tchividjian supposedly once said, 'The deepest fear we have,
"the fear beneath all fears", is the fear of not measuring up, the fear
of judgment. It's this fear that creates the stress and depression of
everyday life.' The more serious press were keen to point out that the
Department for Education were once more guilty of not measuring
up when they had to scrap their plans to test the ability of every
4-year-old in the nation. Many academics had expressed concern
about testing pupils at such a young age. Then suddenly a U-turn
was announced, and schools that had worked hard throughout the

year to develop strategies to implement the tests had to halt their plans because the results were deemed to be unreliable. The response from many professional associations was, 'We told you so.' So the government's latest attempts to disparage teachers had merely put egg all over the face of the hapless Rupert Brinton.[3]

Chapter 14

Leopards, peanuts and compost tip Brian over the hedge

Are YOU a 'grammar Nazi'? You're probably a jerk: language pedants are more likely to be introverted and disagreeable

Daily Mail Online, 1 April 2016

Brian had been planning another early morning meeting with Tom, but in the end that was not possible. A text from the deputy head put paid to that. Brian had to be in school early because Mrs Burton was on the warpath. There were huge tensions between Brian and this particular parent, who was a regular complainant about the treatment 'Our Kylie' received at Springett Lane. Kylie Burton was 8 and she seemed to stumble from one mishap to another, whether it was an accident on the playground or fallings out with other children. Everybody knew when Mrs Burton was on the premises as her shouting could be heard not just at the other end of the school but also the other end of the playground. On one particularly unpleasant occasion, which would have been a cause for concern to the Noise Abatement Society, Brian had reached for Mrs Burton's arm to steer her away from the corridor filled with children towards a quieter part of the school so he could establish the reasons behind this particular outburst. Mrs Burton had shrieked, 'You get your hands off me. That's assault, and I'm reporting you! You are the worst head teacher in this town.' Brian controlled his response, but he had been tempted to retort, 'No, I'm not. The bloke at Megson Grove is much worse than me. He is really rubbish.' But he didn't.

The trouble was that Mrs Burton had great difficulty with words and regularly got them mixed up. Sometimes this made Brian want to snigger at the most inopportune moments. There was the golden moment when she announced that Our Kylie had been to the doctor's and his diagnosis was that she suffered from a 'peanut analogy'. On another occasion, she protested that she was tired of the school treating her child like a leopard and that it was steadily tipping her over the hedge. On this occasion, Kylie had fallen over the previous day and had a swollen knee. Mrs Burton was gunning for Brian because nobody had put cold compost on it, and everybody knows you put cold compost on a swollen knee.

However, it was this conversation that had made Brian start to think further. The simple truth was that Mrs Burton did not lack intelligence, and she could put together a very powerful argument. Sometimes these arguments had made Brian sink lower and lower into his chair as a feeling of dismay swept over him. Mrs Burton's problem was that she lacked confidence with words. Oracy was her stumbling block and potentially it would be the same for many of the children at Springett Lane. Professor David Winkley once said that 'Every person born has six significant talents. Two come to the surface quickly, two are brought out by other people (often teachers) and the other two they take with them to the grave.'[1] Brian knew that his fourth-generation curriculum should help the children to develop new talents, but they also needed to be able to express themselves verbally with confidence. If they could do this, then new doors might open for them in the future. At present, if they found themselves in an interview situation or sought a job that involved customer or client relations, then they may well find those doors closed.

Brian pondered once more. He knew that Tom had worked in many deprived communities, so maybe he had some answers and just a few butterflies to offer. While the opportunity for an early morning visit for coffee and croissants had gone, there was always FaceTime.

Whenever you read a good book, somewhere in the world a door opens to allow in more light[2]

Within about three minutes, Brian had poured out all his thoughts relating to three-generational lessons and the kind of English language curriculum he was trying to create. His outpourings included his numerous conversations with Mrs Burton and the importance of ensuring the children at Springett Lane had the confidence to express themselves verbally in a way that did justice to themselves and the beautiful English language. He dreaded the literacy curriculum becoming focused too heavily on a series of academic grammar and punctuation exercises which could be crudely marked right or wrong.

The FaceTime conversation with Tom was both fascinating and exhilarating. Tom used his considerable knowledge and experience and started by comparing and contrasting the teaching of English over the past century, before moving on to create a new set of butterflies. Tom's greying hair kept sweeping across his face and stubbly chin as he explained there was recent evidence indicating that there had been a sharp fall in children's enjoyment of reading and this was now storing up significant problems for the future. After ten years of the National Literacy Strategy, the National Foundation for Educational Research (NFER) noted that while reading standards had risen (although this could be down to teaching to the test), the percentage of children who enjoyed reading books at the age of 11 had fallen from 70% to 55%. In the obsessive drive to raise standards, the pleasure of reading books may have been irreversibly damaged.[3] As early as 1921, a report had described the process of teaching children to read as being too often a mechanical and deadening process.[4] Yet in some schools today, over a century later, that serious mistake is being repeated.

After a brief pause, Tom showed both his huge academic knowledge and his passion for this aspect of primary education. He rattled off numerous pieces of research which Brian noted down as fast as he could:

* Developing a love of reading can be more important for a child's educational success than their socio-economic background.[5]
* Young children who enjoy reading are nearly five times as likely to read above the expected level for their age.[6]
* Other benefits of reading include an increased vocabulary, pleasure in reading in later life, a better

understanding of other cultures and a greater insight into human nature.[7]

* In schools that have success with their pupils' reading standards, teachers read, talk with enthusiasm and recommend books, the results of which are not only seen in test results but also in an enthusiasm for reading which extends beyond the classroom.[8]

* In too many schools there is not enough time given to wider reading for pleasure.[9]

Tom went on to say that the answer lies in greater use of both story time and popular culture, stressing the importance of making sure that every day includes high quality story time and that the teachers know the stories and read or tell them well. He considered that Rupert Brinton needed to learn the words of Kate DiCamillo who apparently said, 'Reading should not be presented to children as a chore or duty. It should be offered as a precious gift.'

Tom continued: 'I see Rupert Brinton wants the children to be absorbed in the classics from a very early stage.[10] Well, you could do that, and I've seen some splendid work from such sources. However, if I were you, I would leave that until later and start by using high quality, contemporary children's fiction. Use books and stories that have won recent awards. If you do that, you will truly be moving in the opposite direction to the secretary of state. As a starting point, don't use anything more than 15 years old.' Brian scribbled down the words as fast as he could:

Too many teachers are using the books they grew up with, and if this carries on we will still be reading Charlie and the Chocolate Factory to children in another hundred years' time. Children need stories that include the internet and mobile phones so they can explore issues such as, 'What is a good use of the internet?' and 'What is a bad use of the internet?' to ensure they develop an understanding of cyberbullying.

Teachers should regularly use local stories, or stories that use accent and dialect, to add to their appreciation of

the richness of the English language. This also provides a clear sense of identity for the children.

Schools should draw up a list of really rich stories that are age appropriate for the youngsters who make up Generation Z, including what is good about our world and what needs to change. In that way, we can use fiction to demonstrate how humans can act for both good and ill towards their fellows. Schools should use stories about how brave people overcome adversity to bring about change.

After nourishment, shelter and companionship, stories are the things we need most in the world[11]

There was a pause, and there needed to be. Brian could barely keep pace with Tom's butterflies. As he put his final full stop in place, Tom picked up speed once more, saying, 'If schools are going to promote a genuine love of reading, these are the questions they should ask.'

* Is the reading stock updated regularly with children being involved in the process?
* Can less able readers access books without feeling marginalised?
* Does the school's library and book stock include current bestsellers?
* Are reading displays regularly revitalised to encourage reading and develop interests?
* Is it clear that non-fiction books can be read for pleasure?
* Can readers sit comfortably to read?
* Can the full class sit in the reading area?
* Are e-books and other types of technology present?
* Are magazines and other reading materials readily available?
* Is there a range of books in the classroom relating to a current theme?
* Do books in classrooms reflect an appropriate range of ability?
* Are the winners and nominees of national book awards identified and their works promoted?

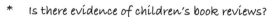

* Is there evidence of children's book reviews?
* Are the children's top reads identified?
* Is there a selection of the teacher's own books present?
* Is stock rotated and displayed in an inviting way?
* Do teachers read full stories skilfully to wide-eyed children?
* Do teachers read opening paragraphs of several books, leaving them as cliffhangers?
* Do teachers show the children covers of books and get them to predict what they are about?
* Do teachers read key incidents from books to promote interest?
* Do teachers share pictures from books and ask the children for their predictions about the story?
* Do they celebrate World Book Day and National Poetry Day?

After another pause Tom continued by saying, 'We do not learn to drive in order to understand the workings of the internal combustion engine and the procedures identified in the Highway Code. We learn to drive in order to open up our world and seek new opportunities. We don't learn to read to understand grammatical conventions but to open up our world to the fantastic pleasure and opportunities books bring.'

'Wow, that's a brilliant statement that conjures up precisely what I believe!' said Brian, who then went on to ask, 'Did you just make that up?'

'No, I didn't,' replied Tom. 'Somebody who was very wise said it, though I can't remember who.'[12]

Tom said, 'Here comes another thought: teachers should use popular culture more, whether it be through the films they see, the television programmes they watch or the music they listen to. When that is done well, inadvertently you will be introducing children to the world of sociolinguistics and language registers.'

Tom concluded that the mere term 'sociolinguistics' should be enough to annoy dear old Rupert Brinton and send shudders down his spine. However, if used well, it would give the children a confidence with spoken language and prevent them from becoming the next Mrs Burton.

Brian had no idea what either sociolinguistics or language registers were, but he knew he had to find out.

The spoken word belongs half to him who speaks it and half to him who listens[13]

By the following morning, Brian knew that if the children at Springett Lane Primary School were to develop a sense of aspiration and find the doors of opportunity being opened to them, then language registers were the answer. Rather than dull, unimaginative academic exercises involving the children correcting grammar and punctuation mistakes, this would be the way forward. To clarify his thoughts further, he even found support from the unusual source of the *Daily Telegraph*, which reported that those who are obsessed with correcting the grammar of others are likely to be rather dull and introverted people who lack confidence in themselves.[14] The ill-considered ramblings of the secretary of state had the capacity to create a generation of teachers with these same hang-ups. Brian recalled his previous thoughts about grammar snobs and thought that the last thing the children at Springett Lane wanted or needed were teachers who were introverted or disagreeable.

Brian knew that when people become successful in life, a key element is usually their command of spoken English. The reality is that we need to be able to use a wide range of different language styles. Following his conversation with Tom he now knew these were sometimes called registers. We would not speak in the same way during a formal interview as we would if we were sharing a drink with friends at the local pub. Brian knew it would be difficult to imagine the BBC newsreader who is a master of Received Pronunciation using the same style of speech while witnessing a controversial incident among friends at his favourite football club. He knew that adapting the way you speak on a particular topic or in a particular situation should be a relatively straightforward matter. However, to many of the pupils at Springett Lane, it wasn't. They may have been geniuses at native English, but the truth is that many entered school with low language skills and lacked confidence in spoken English. The constant correcting of their use of language would be having a negative demotivating effect. By contrast, exploring and having fun with the range of language registers would equip the learners with a key life skill. Brian started to write:

Developing the formal language register: Children need to be able to speak well in a formal situation – for example, when they are presenting something. They may need to use technical vocabulary. The discourse will be one way, without interruptions. The children need mastery of the formal language register to hold the attention of an audience.

Developing the consultative language register: Children need to be able to interact with others in order to seek understanding or to find solutions. This may involve discussing background information. This is a language register that is essential in adult life. Examples would include a doctor and patient talking or an expert talking to an apprentice. It would therefore be acceptable to use phrases such as, 'Uh huh' or 'I see'. However, it could also be a conversation between two equals who have a problem to solve.

Developing the casual language register: This will enable the children to mix with their friends in a social context. Dialect, slang or the use of nicknames may be common. The conversation may not be based around full sentences and ellipses will take place. People will readily interrupt each other to join the conversation. This will be important in equipping the children to make and sustain friendships or simply have fun.

Developing the intimate language register: The children need to be able to communicate at an intimate level with members of their family or to build a special relationship. On these occasions, intonation and body language (including eye contact) can be key elements of success.

Developing the frozen language register: This is a very static form of language. It is often read out from a script in a systematic way. The words and intonation are set and do not change. It could be used by the announcer at a *railway station, a police officer reading a caution or when making a pledge.*[15]

Brian knew that if the children could explore language registers in an exciting and fun way, so they could use each one with confidence, he would be providing them with a far greater life skill than the ability to underline a verb in an unimaginative sentence. The question was, how could he do this? Suddenly an email pinged in from Eve which helped to provide the answer:

Hi Bri,

Just read an interesting report on the state of education in Chicago which is being replicated in many US states. The Chicago Public Schools system continues to embrace a high stakes testing policy. As a result of these methods, a school with low reading scores would be placed on probation with the threat of being closed down and having its staff dismissed or reassigned. The state has also done away with 'social promotion' and now every child in the third, sixth and eighth grade has to achieve a minimum score on the standardised test known as the Iowa Test of Basic Skills.

All good for accountability you may think, but the reality is that high stakes testing simply led to high stakes cheating, as schools across Chicago tried to fool the system. Some teachers were accused of helping students or changing answers. There were unusual patterns of success in the answers to the harder questions when some young people had got easier questions wrong or even missed them out. As a result, when the scores went up it was attributed to good teaching rather than manipulating the test, and if the scores went down it was attributed to poor teaching. As a consequence, poor teachers were sometimes being promoted, with good teachers dismissed or choosing to leave their profession.[16]

The effects proved to be demoralising, with teaching standards becoming mediocre and terrified teachers just teaching and re-teaching certain pieces of information 'justin case' it came up on the test.

I don't think there is a place for someone like you in Chicago. They would see you as a dangerous radical. That's a shame because it seems to me that it is the director of public schools who is the dangerous radical because he seems hell-bent on eradicating those good schools that dare to be different and where children learn without limits.

There may be no place for you in Chicago, but the sun, sea and sand here are spectacular. Come and see me soon, Brian. I miss you!

Eve x

Several things struck Brian as a result of reading the email. First, there was that reinvigorating message that he needed to dare to be different and that children needed to learn without limits. Second, the dangers of an over-emphasis on testing were clearly spelled out. Third, he was intrigued by the typographical error where 'justin' and the unexpected use of inverted commas had been used instead of simply writing 'just in'. Brian wondered if he should correct this part of the email and send it back to Eve, but that would simply make him an introverted 'grammar Nazi'. Finally, he thought that maybe he should go out to California and see if he could rekindle his relationship with Eve, but first he needed to focus on that typographical error (or not) because, strangely, that was about to help him create a very special type of teacher.

Brian's mind was whirring as he invented two fictional but very contrasting teachers. The second of these would be precisely what he needed to promote language registers and teach three-generational lessons within a fourth-generation curriculum at Springett Lane.

Mr Justin Case

Mr Justin Case was the type of teacher Rupert Brinton would love to see in schools across the country, therefore he was exactly the type of teacher Brian didn't want at Springett Lane. Justin Case was the type of teacher who saw it as his (or her) job to stand in front of a class and authoritatively impart knowledge to children sitting in rows, wearing crisp blazers and passively recording key pieces of information in their neatly presented exercise books. If the children were undertaking a project on Tudor Britain they would be taught the key dates, the names of the monarchs and the six wives of Henry VIII, and the reason for this would be 'just in case' they needed this information at a later stage. Brian himself had been schooled in this way, and had even been taught that the former capital of the Belgian colony of the Congo was Léopold-ville, just in case he ever needed to know. To date he had never needed this information.

Brian was in no way opposed to direct teaching. All children need to experience direct teaching in order to provide them with the basic skills they need for life. As a teacher and head teacher, Brian knew that discovery favours the well-prepared mind. If the children at Springett Lane were going to produce the beautiful work he sought, he knew that they had to learn the craftsmanship of being a scholar. While Brian knew that he wanted to think more about the aspect of craftsmanship, he now moved his mind away from Mr Justin Case, because he was about to invent the truly inspi-rational Miss Justine Tyme.

Miss Justine Tyme

Miss Justine Tyme was the sort of teacher Rupert Brinton would hate to see in schools across the country, therefore she was exactly the type of teacher Brian did want at Springett Lane. Miss Tyme's approach was different. At the start of a term she would stand in front of her class and tell the children that they were about to start a project relating to, say, Tudor Britain. They would need a very exciting 'wow' start to their study, so they would be told that at the conclusion of the project they would be running a museum for a day. Not only would they invite parents and grandparents to the museum but also the local press and the lord mayor. Because the children would be displaying their work to such an eminent audi-ence, Miss Tyme would go on to tell the children that it needed to be of the very highest standard. As a consequence, there would be occasions when she would use direct teaching to impart knowledge or teach a significant skill. However, in the museum for a day there would also be an opportunity for the children to carry out their own research and make interactive presentations or fulfil the 'mantle of the expert'. The children could make short films about Tudor life or dress up and perform short plays. They could learn to create portraits of Tudor monarchs for the displays within their museum. To ensure their museum was a great success story, they would take greater responsibility for shaping their own learning, and it would be the role of the teacher to ensure that the students received the appropriate teaching and learning opportunities just in time (rather than just in case).

Brian knew that if he could create a team of Justine Tyme teachers then he could genuinely develop classrooms where true learning without limits took place. In addition to having a thorough knowledge of Tudor Britain, they would also develop key personal learning and thinking skills as team workers, creative thinkers, independent enquirers and effective participators.[17] The classroom would become like a giant talent show as the children rose to the fore in their different ways, some as actors, others as writers, artists or filmmakers. Above everything else, they would have the opportunity to use some of the key language registers. Children could be taught about how to use the formal language register when they took up the mantle of the expert. They could be taught about the consultative language register as they negotiated with and tried to influence each other. Through the use of announcements there would be opportunities to use the frozen register. There would also be countless opportunities to use the casual language register along the way. This only left the intimate language register. Brian thought long and hard about this and decided perhaps he had better try this himself. He reached for his mobile phone and dialled. There seemed to be a long delay before anybody answered. 'Hello Andrea,' said Brian nervously. 'I was wondering if we could meet up. I wanted to talk to you about my last text.'

Melting Andrea's frozen language register

The telephone conversation lasted for a good forty-five minutes. It was difficult and frosty at the start. Brian almost recognised a frozen language register but didn't know why until Andrea explained that she had returned to the wine bar and seen him in deep conversation with someone else. After Brian explained what had happened a more casual language register developed.

After their conversation ended, Brian looked down at his notes once more. He had moved a considerable distance with his work on

producing a rich and vivid language curriculum, but he knew he hadn't really addressed that tricky issue of how to teach grammar and punctuation in a way that would keep his political masters happy. However, he also knew that it could wait for the time being. He had something more important to do. He was meeting up with Andrea because they were going to plan a weekend away in the Cotswolds. This time it was Andrea who made a rash decision. She had suggested that as she was short of cash, perhaps they could share a room. Brian knew this might be problematic but also knew that it would provide a good chance to talk.

More bad news at the coasting department

Meanwhile there was further misfortune for the unlucky Rupert Brinton. The press were keen to report on yet another major error in his department – which probably cost the nation a small fortune while his government pursued a policy of austerity. The Standards and Testing Agency managed to publish online the spelling, punctuation and grammar test designed for 7-year-olds long before the date of the test. This was described as 'an unfortunate human error'. The press were quick to point out that over the last fifteen years, people often referred to as the 'Key Stage Cops' had been employed to patrol schools and check that test papers were locked away securely in sealed packages in school safes and stockrooms.[18] The blunder occurred only weeks after the government had been forced to abandon its controversial tests for 5-year-olds for comparability reasons. It really did look like the hapless Mr Brinton was leading a coasting and somewhat clumsy Department for Education, leaving schools to cope with the chaos that ensued.

A longer term review might have concluded that surely things couldn't get much worse. We had reached the stage where the Department for Education was experiencing a crisis of confidence. It was on a war footing and being run like a sitcom. There were alleged complaints about bullying being rife. Some parents had accused the secretary of state of having breathtaking arrogance and others suggested he was mixing business with pleasure. There was evidence that government policies could lead to a generation of physically and mentally unhealthy children. Potential bias had been identified in the inspection system in order to support specific government initiatives. New policies were preventing many children from receiving an education whereby all their talents could be recognised and developed, therefore they were not getting a rounded education. Messages coming from the Department for Education were described as confusing and this was leading to a culture of fear and uncertainty. Now schools were facing a situation where tests were being cancelled or abandoned.

Many people might have wondered if Rupert Brinton really was a suitable person to be secretary of state for education. The prime minister clearly thought he was.

Chapter 15
This way to the nuclear bunker and other secrets

Stop using so many exclamation marks!!! New guidelines warn pupils to stop misusing punctuation

Daily Mail Online, 6 March 2016

The trouble with having good ideas is that they give you an initial burst of energy before the self-doubt starts to creep in. As Brian made his way to the wine bar, he was uncertain about whether or not he was doing the right thing at Springett Lane. His ideas about producing an exciting English language curriculum were now becoming well-formed but nagging fears were starting to intrude. He wondered if it wouldn't be better just to play it safe and forget about some of his ideas. He still hadn't worked out a clear approach to teaching grammar and punctuation, and he knew the popular educational publishers had produced many schemes that he could simply buy into. They would make life much easier and the teachers would probably prefer it because it would simply remove the pressure. Additionally, there was still no sign of Brian finding a way to teach mathematics in a new and exciting way that the dreaded Rupert Brinton would wish to rail against. However, in the meantime, Brian had a more pleasant distraction. He was off to meet Andrea.

After an uncertain start the conversation flowed and so did the wine. The initial bottle of Pinot Grigio quickly disappeared and a much more expensive bottle of Prosecco followed. The conversation lightened and, before long, they were planning their weekend away in the Cotswolds. But as the third glass of Prosecco was poured

Brian glazed over once more. One of the features of working as an educational leader is that you can never totally switch off. As a skilled leadership expert, Andrea recognised the signs and moved the conversation towards reassuring Brian.

She looked into his eyes and said, 'I'm going to tell you a story, Brian. It will only last a few moments and then we are going back to planning our weekend away. Last week, I was working in Essex and had to drive from Brentwood to Dagenham. As I was starting my journey, I looked up and saw a most unusual road sign. It was one of those brown tourist signs and it pointed the way to "The Secret Nuclear Bunker". I smiled and thought to myself, "That is the best street sign ever – and not only that it sums up leadership." Great leaders take their organisations to a place they shouldn't normally access, including secret nuclear bunkers!'

After a pause, Andrea continued the tale of her journey through Essex: 'By the time I had travelled along the A13 and was approaching Dagenham, I knew I was getting closer to the Ford car factory. I found myself thinking about the striking female workers in 1968 who campaigned for equal pay for women. They caused a real stir in political circles at the time and their contribution to equality was brought to the public's attention in 2010 through the film *Made in Dagenham*. Their story was told through a ficti-tious leader called Rita O'Grady, who was really an amalgam of the real-life protagonists, including Rose Boland, the strike leader. The then employment secretary, Barbara Castle, described her as a formidable leader. There is no doubt that she, along with her imme-diate colleagues, was an inside out leader driven by the strong moral purpose of securing equal pay and working rights for women.[1] As a consequence, they brought about considerable change. They were driven by an extremely strong belief, and schools need leaders with the same sense of purpose. It seems to me that too many schools are doing what they are told without real commitment and to a mediocre standard, while others do what they believe in with energy and to an incredible standard.' Brian added her final words to his notebook along with a quotation Andrea used from Confucius:

Do not worry because you have no official position.
Worry about your qualifications. Do not worry because

no one appreciates your abilities. Seek to be worthy of appreciation.[2]

She then added:

Failure is never quite as frightening as regret.[3]

As promised, Andrea then moved the conversation back to their forthcoming mini-break and announced, 'I was a little bit shocked when you asked me to come to the Cotswolds. I really didn't know what to say, but then I decided it was just like receiving a gift from Father Christmas. But, of course, you don't believe in Father Christmas, do you?'

'No,' replied Brian, 'I still don't believe in Father Christmas.'

'Well you should, because those who believe in magic will live a magical life.'

The minister for exclamation marks

A glance at the newspapers the following morning revealed the government's intention to stop children from using an exclamation mark unless the sentence began with 'what' or 'how'. Brian thought of the many problems facing the world that the government seemed unprepared to tackle. He thought of the huge corporations that refused to pay anything like their fair share of tax. He thought about the challenges of living in rapidly changing communities. He thought of people fleeing war zones. In many of these examples governance had been weak or inadequate, and yet there was clear evidence of strong governance when it came to the use of the exclamation mark. However, government ministers had done precious little when it came to promoting a generation of children who would be excited writers who could take a piece of paper and produce something as beautiful and valuable as white gold.

Brian then realised that was precisely what Anne Moody's class of children had been doing by the old canal. They had become real writers and turned their paper into white gold – and, strangely, they seemed to have no problems with punctuation or grammar.

The notion of excited writers made Brian turn to the bookshelves once more to reach for another of those books from yesteryear with a cloth cover. The volume was *The Excitement of Writing*, written by Sir Alec Clegg, who, in his time, had been the highly influential chief education officer in the West Riding of Yorkshire.[4] Clegg was a man who left a clear legacy of pupil creativity around the challenging communities that made up the South Yorkshire coalfields. Tom had frequently referred to Clegg's work. He had met the 'great man', as he called him, in his formative years and had often mentioned that one day he would like to write a biography of Clegg before his thoughts and ideas were lost forever. Brian found the passage he had been looking for:

> Each year schools of all kinds spend at least many hundreds of thousands of pounds on books of English exercises designed to prepare pupils for external exercises such as the Eleven Plus selection test, the O and A levels of the GCE and even exams that are not yet fully operative such as the Certificate of Secondary Education. And in a survey of schools it was found that those producing the most sensitive work did not use these exercises but in many cases considered their use harmful.[5]

He looked down at one of the examples of work produced by Anne Moody's class and read it once more. Their writing was certainly sensitive and enriched by the creative use of the English language. Additionally, the grammar, spelling and punctuation clearly added to its beauty. Brian knew he needed to know more. However, he also knew that this could lead to yet another uncomfortable meeting with Anne Moody. He finished the last dregs of his coffee and set off for school.

Daniel, Thirkettles pork pies, Estonia and £150 in used fivers

An hour or so later, Brian was heading down the corridor to organise his meeting with Anne Moody when his mind was totally distracted by the sight of 9-year-old Daniel Taylor hurtling towards him with a fistful of £5 notes. The sight of Daniel with money was most disturbing. His family never contributed to the costs of educational visits, and he had frequently been caught stealing both money and other items from children's bags. This was often done simply to try to buy the friends he was desperately seeking. Daniel was lonely and unkempt, with much of the former contents of his nose smeared across his school sweatshirt. While Brian often felt sorry for Daniel, he also knew it was unwise to trust him near money. He was never asked to take the class dinner money to the school office for fear that he would stop and count it into two piles: 'One for me and one for you …'

Brian looked at Daniel and knew that it was wrong in principle to be so suspicious, but that didn't stop him confronting the boy and asking him what he was doing with the money. Brian then realised that he had indeed been wrong to be suspicious. In reality, it was one of those moments when a head teacher pulls out his or her hair and thinks, 'How come I never fully seem to know what is happening in this place?' The response from Daniel did nothing to clarify the situation, as it seemed that the money related, in some form, to Thirkettles pork pies and Estonia. While Brian knew that Rob Thirkettle owned the local butcher's shop and they frequently won awards for their meat pies which were distributed countrywide, he wasn't sure why there would be any kind of link to Estonia. In truth, Brian didn't really know where Estonia was. On impulse he rerouted himself and walked alongside Daniel who was still tightly clutching £150 in used £5 notes as he moved towards his classroom. They parted at the classroom door.

Brian's mobile phone pinged indicating that an email had just arrived from Eve. While he wouldn't normally have read a social email during the school day, he felt in need of a light diversion. However he was aware that there were still many questions to be answered relating to Daniel, pork pies, Estonia and £150 in used fivers.

I hope one day when I say I'm from Estonia, people don't say, 'What? Where's that?'[6]

Brian opened his phone and started to read Eve's email:

Hi Bri,

I have spent the last year trying to entice you to the upbeat Silicon Valley of California, but sadly you have rejected my every move. I know why. There is an even more exciting place than northern California and it makes us look like laggards. So I am considering joining the most advanced digital society in the world. If I hand over 50 euros and a photograph I can have my fingerprints taken, and after my credentials have been checked I will be issued with an identity card, a cryptographic key, a PIN code and access to its national systems, because I would be an official e-resident of Estonia. You ought to find out more about this remarkable place. It could help your work, and Rupert Brinton would absolutely hate it.

Estonia is a nation that only looks forward and the changes over the last twenty-five years have been phenomenal. In 1991 only half the country had a phone line, but by 1997 97% of schools were online. By 2000 cabinet meetings had gone paperless. By 2002 the government had built a free Wi-Fi network covering nearly every populated area. By 2001 e-voting had been introduced. By 2012 huge networks of ultra-fast fibre-optic cables were being laid and now 94% of tax returns are filed online.

And not only that, this relatively new nation performs well in the PISA educational rankings. Perhaps we should both go and take a look. What do you say, Brian? How about a romantic encounter in Estonia with a little work thrown in?

Eve x

The Estonian link was there once more. Brian was getting more and more intrigued, especially if there was something to be learned, and even more so if whatever it was he learned would annoy the dastardly Rupert Brinton.

A quick glance at the PISA rankings indicated that Estonia did perform well in the international league tables, especially in mathematics. A quote from former US President Barack Obama charted other successes: 'Estonia is one of the great success stories among the nations that reclaimed their independence after the Cold War. You've built a vibrant democracy and new prosperity, and you've become a model for how citizens can interact with their government in the 21st century, something President Ilves has championed. With their digital IDs, Estonians can use their smartphones to get just about anything done online, from their children's

grades to their health records. I should have called the Estonians when we were setting up our healthcare website.'[7]

Brian was reading aloud a quotation from Carmen Kass: 'You know what I always dreamed of? That with the greenhouse effect, one day Estonia can be what Los Angeles is right now. I always thought when the end of the world comes, I want to be in Estonia. I think then I'd survive.' Brian said to himself, 'Well, you can go to Estonia, but I'm off to Essex – apparently there is a secret nuclear bunker there.' Then suddenly he glazed over as once again he became concerned for his sanity. Brian's capacity to talk to himself was certainly on the increase and now he seemed to want to put himself in a secret nuclear bunker. 'Maybe I am going mad,' he said to the empty room.

Just then there was a knock at the door. Alice and Alicia from Year 1, who seemed to be joined at the hip, stood there sweetly holding hands and politely saying, 'Miss Walker says we can't find the seed box. Do you know where it is?' Brian was delighted that Miss Walker was starting to take outdoor education seriously by taking the children outside to do some gardening. Brian told them to leave it to him and he would go and find it.

Two lost hours later, with just a little cursing along the way, the tin box containing a range of seed packets had been found. The sun was still shining and there was time for the children to go to the school allotment. Brian loved the idea of young children experiencing the magic of seeing beautiful things grow. Brian proudly walked in and announced, 'Here's the seed box'. Miss Walker looked at the packets of assorted vegetable seeds and said, 'No, I wanted the CD box. We needed the music for assembly.'

Two lost hours and a class of children staring at worksheets while so many learning opportunities existed outside on a glorious sunny day. Brian was now feeling really low and there was still the Moody woman to see. While he wanted to have the conversation with her, he also knew it could be awkward after their meeting in the wine bar. He left the room chuntering under his breath, 'What was it Lindy West said, "We only get one life. Wasting someone's time is the subtlest form of murder"?'[8] Brian knew that the same thoughts must have crossed the minds of hundreds of other head teachers.

The craftsmanship of being a scholar

Brian had a sense that the meeting with Anne Moody would also be a waste of time. It wasn't. The start was slow and clumsy, but fortunately there were still samples of the children's work spread out on the desks in front of them. Anne could see that Brian was puzzled. How could she have achieved such quality, and what form of transformation had taken place?

Once again, she took the initiative and started to speak: 'Since 1998 there has been wave after wave of central initiatives. I have not believed in many of them and I felt as though my identity as a teacher diminished along with my confidence and my self-esteem. I knew I had become dull and boring. I didn't have the courage to dare to be different because, if I did, I could lose my job. Now my strategy is to stand firm, and if that makes me different to the rest, then so be it. I decided it had to be my way or no way. So I went back to basics, but the basics of what *I* want to stand for. However, the difference is that now you seem to have come looking for my advice and that seems like quite a turnaround, especially as for the last decade successive head teachers have chosen to ignore me rather than speak to me. That's wrong. Surely it is the job of the leader to invest intellectual capital in their staff and help shape their practice and beliefs?'

There was a period of silence while the terms of Henry Stewart's *The Happy Manifesto* came back into Brian's mind, as well as the three signs of a miserable job that had been identified by Patrick Lencioni. He then picked up another piece of the children's writing and once more looked at how they had used their senses and grappled and played with the vocabulary in order to strive for quality. He imagined the children's conversations as they tried, rejected and sought out new phrases. He started to read:

A Hidden World Made by Nature Itself
    The stems of the branches were as sharp as daggers. You could imagine venom in them. Torturing spikes lean out and seek to grab you, wearing a purple coat around their claw. One twisted knotted tree hands you a bouquet of flowers and leaves. This is a hidden world made by nature itself. You can imagine fairies, pixies and elves

playing by the water at the edge of the old canal. When I felt one of the leaves snake around my foot goosebumps trickled down my spine.

The first glimpse of water caught my eye as it slowly swished from side to side. Every movement was like a delicate flower in the wind. The trees leaned over to try and grab a sip of the water. Nearby workers took a break as the rain clouds started to cry. Graffiti was daubed on the old brick walls. Decorated trams could be seen snaking along their journey behind the jungle-like trees.

McKayla and Chloe[9]

After a pause Brian spoke, saying, 'It seems to me that Rupert Brinton wants to turn primary education into a pass or fail situation, where our children simply do more and more tests with more and more questions that they will either get right or wrong. It feels like education is becoming a training programme for children to be able to compete against the test paper. You say you want to do it differently, and I want to do it differently to Rupert Brinton, and this feels very different. So maybe we should dare to do it differently together.'

Brian thought once more about the craftsmanship of being a scholar. He started to write as Anne Moody spoke about how she sought to develop a culture of excellence:

Agree	Creating excellence and the craftsmanship of being a scholar	Disagree
	The approach is based on every adult and every child succeeding and believing they should help others succeed.	
	It should not be about merely completing the task but more about every child achieving a beautiful, high quality outcome.	
	To do this children have to learn the craftsmanship of being a scholar and recognise their classroom as the workshop where they strive for excellence.	

Agree	Creating excellence and the craftsmanship of being a scholar	Disagree
	Once a project is underway, it is the duty of everyone to ensure that everybody succeeds.	
	We strive for a situation where we can achieve a whole class sense of pride and the sense of a job well done.	
	The work will be celebrated, displayed and put into portfolios of the children's best work. Their achievements will reflect: • Pride and perseverance. • Originality and uniqueness. • Independence and collaboration. • Applying prior learning. • Responding positively to feedback.	

Brian added the columns to the left and right at a later stage. He thought the statements from Anne Moody could make a brilliant professional development activity, whereby staff could consider each statement in turn and place an arrow in the appropriate column to indicate whether they agreed or disagreed with the statement. They could make their arrows long or short in order to depict how much they agreed or disagreed.

There was no doubt that the strategy could help the children to believe that a piece of white paper could indeed become a piece of white gold because of the beauty it now contained. However, there was still a problem with a government that seemed hell-bent on turning the assessment of English into a measure of something that was either right or wrong. The teaching of grammar and punctuation was potentially unaddressed by Anne Moody's approach.

The past is always tense and the future, perfect[10]

Brian asked the question directly: 'The way in which the children use grammar and punctuation is really good. How was this achieved?'

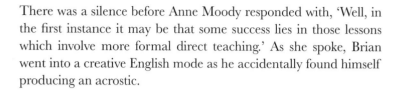

There was a silence before Anne Moody responded with, 'Well, in the first instance it may be that some success lies in those lessons which involve more formal direct teaching.' As she spoke, Brian went into a creative English mode as he accidentally found himself producing an acrostic.

In the essential art of direct teaching, the teacher:

* Decides the outcomes.
* Identifies the steps.
* Refines the language as necessary to gain optimum learning.
* Engages the heart because that will make the learning last.
* Checks the learning by constantly assessing what is going on.
* Tunes and tweaks the lesson to attain excellence.

Brian looked at his notes and felt pleased with what he had written, especially as not only had he created an acrostic but he had also referred to direct teaching as an art. Brian thought back to the mythical Justine Tyme, the primary practitioner who brought the art and science of pedagogy together. He remembered the need to think in ink and reached again for his pen:

Great teaching happens when a skilled practitioner brings together the science and the art of pedagogy.

Brian's feeling of smugness was now starting to replace his earlier unease. Before long, Anne Moody continued to answer his question: 'However, direct teaching is only part of the answer to how the children used grammar and punctuation in their writing. Before we went to the canal, we had a practice in the school grounds. The children developed a whole range of exciting phrases using powerful adjectives, similes and metaphors. Then we sat around the flip chart and constructed a whole class description of the scene with the view that it could be used as a story setting. While the children helped by producing stunning vocabulary, the grammar and punctuation was all over the place. So then we sat and looked at the flip chart and used everything we had learned about punctuation and grammar to produce an exciting descriptive story setting that the reader could become totally absorbed in.' She handed over the collaboratively produced text:

Once Upon a Summer's Day

As I scout around by the weather demolished greenhouse I feel the soft summer breeze sprint past my face. Cotton clouds shaped like dragons, ducks and distant angels are creating dramatic scenes of falling princesses and ancient warriors high above. Tall, spikey, neglected weeds are waiting for their prey. The fresh lush emerald grass, which was coated in a thin layer of emerald dew, swished in the warm breeze. The sounds of children echoed through my eardrums. Energetic youngsters who looked like a swarm of uniformed black and yellow striped wasps played contentedly in the playground. The class down in the foundation stage ran around in circles like bees around the sweet nectar of a fluorescent flower. The sounds of the children suddenly stopped after the shrill scream of a whistle filled the air.

Mrs Sharp strutted across the field with great splendour and authority, while our teacher patrolled the area like a hawk watching its prey. With intense concentration she leaned towards the future authors with interest. Across the field children walked into a bigger group listening intently to what would happen next, as the trees danced wildly in the summer breeze. The class then walked away and into school.

Mrs Sharp reached into her pocket and took out her mobile phone in order to ...[11]

After Brian had read the text, taking time to spot the alliteration, onomatopoeia, similes and metaphors, Anne Moody continued to speak: 'The whole process equipped the children to produce their own writing and set the expectations. It also gave them the sense that they were all responsible for ensuring the success of everybody else. While I circulated to ensure all the children were fully engaged in the task, periodically they offered each other praise and feedback. When I trained to teach I learned that discovery favours the well-prepared mind and that you need to provide both direct teaching and the opportunities for children to express themselves creatively.'

There was that phrase again about discovery favouring the well-prepared mind. Frighteningly, it seemed that Brian had more in common with Anne Moody then he had ever realised. As he continued to listen, he suddenly found another acrostic coming on that, once again, stressed how in the best lessons the science and the art of pedagogy work hand in hand.

When learning is inspirational the child:

* Imagines because the heart and mind is stimulated.
* Negotiates and navigates the range of possibilities.
* Selects the best route to an outcome of genuine value.
* Perseveres with presentation, which is considered from the start.
* Immerses themselves in the activity.
* Reflects and refines as they go along.
* Evaluates in some form, which is essential.

Tom had told Brian of the power of creating classrooms that were hubs of excellence as an exciting way of providing inspirational professional development. He knew that the approach fitted within the terms of *The Happy Manifesto*. Brian had a new dilemma. Should Anne Moody, who had been a scourge ever since he had taken up the post, become the first teacher to lead a 'hub of excellence'? Brian wasn't certain he knew the answer. It certainly seemed that she had become a revitalised and dynamic teacher who was simply doing what she passionately believed in. Brian also knew that her new enthusiasm could become contagious when talking to others. Brian stood up to leave, but he looked back at Anne Moody one more time. He ran his fingers through his hair and said, 'So you think we should be teaching children to produce beautiful work in all subjects in the curriculum?'

She didn't look up as she replied, 'I believe it was Laetitia Casta who said the creation of beauty is an art. I think all subjects have a beauty – each and every one.'

'How about mathematics?' retorted Brian.

This time she looked him square in the eye and said, 'Especially mathematics. Mathematics is the most beautiful subject in the world. Wasn't it Einstein who said that mathematics was "the poetry of logical ideas"? Number and shape are filled with the most beautiful patterns. Mathematics is like the journey of a river: it starts with the smallest steps and if the journey reaches its conclusion, it ends in magnificence. Mr Smith, you are forever writing things in that notebook of yours. Pass me a clean page and I will show you the beauty of mathematics.' This time it was Anne Moody's turn to write in Brian's notebook:

$$1 \times 8 + 1 = 9$$
$$12 \times 8 + 2 = 98$$
$$123 \times 8 + 3 = 987$$
$$1234 \times 8 + 4 = 9876$$
$$12345 \times 8 + 5 = 98765$$
$$123456 \times 8 + 6 = 987654$$
$$1234567 \times 8 + 7 = 9876543$$
$$12345678 \times 8 + 8 = 98765432$$
$$123456789 \times 8 + 9 = 987654321$$

'How is that for a beautiful pattern of shape and number?'

Brian moved to observe what Anne Moody had written, and said, 'Rupert Brinton says we should look towards Shanghai's methods; the *Daily Mail* says we should ditch trendy teaching methods for chalk and talk.'

Anne Moody's response was, 'You surprise me, Mr Smith, I didn't have you down as a *Daily Mail* reader. I thought you would be more of a *Guardian* man.'

'I am,' replied Brian.

'Then look to Estonia. We have all been finding out about Estonia. We have been doing it and plotting behind your back, Mr Smith. We have all been daring to be different to see if you noticed. You should join in and you might find beautiful mathematics!'

Disappearing vulnerable children at risk in twenty-first century England

As a reader of *The Guardian*, Brian had been appalled and disgusted to learn about the high rates of pupil exclusions that were taking place across the nation as schools apparently sought to increase their ranking in school league tables. In January 2016, the newspaper reported that 10,000 secondary students appeared to have left schools in the run-up to their GCSE examinations.[12] Back in 2013–2014, 2,880 pupils were permanently excluded from secondary schools, with the numbers peaking in Year 10 as examinations approached. Two-thirds of these had special educational needs. A significant proportion were excluded from the government's favoured academy chains. The head of Ofsted expressed concerns that it was not clear where the excluded pupils were being educated and that in some cases they could be at risk of harm. During the same period, primary school exclusions also rose, and the school's minister considered this to be a great success because it was evident that giving increased powers to primary heads was paying off.[13]

Chapter 16
Real mathematics is based in the real world

Every child will have to know their tables off by heart by the age of 11 in government 'war on innumeracy'

Daily Mail Online, 3 January 2016

Brian awoke in a bad mood. The *Daily Mail* headline was only a part of the problem. The government had now decided that even more testing was needed and this time it would be multiplication tables. He scowled and muttered under his breath, 'If only schools had thought of multiplication tables we could have been ahead of the game.' As he read the story, he realised there appeared to be a significant flaw in Rupert Brinton's plan. He claimed that he was waging a war on innumeracy in schools, yet standards in mental arithmetic had *risen* each year over a six-year period. Therefore, imposing a tables test seemed, in an era the government called 'austerity', to be poor value for money.

Poor value for money! Now that was the second reason Brian had woken in a bad mood. He glanced down at the home insurance renewal notice that had risen by 30% since the previous year as a result of a claim for a leaking pipe. Brian (and the insurance company) realised that the easiest thing for him to do was absolutely nothing and accept the new terms. However, there is a very old joke that says a Yorkshireman's answer to any question is 'How much?'

As a result, Brian had decided to set aside a couple of hours for ringing around various companies and brokers in order to get a better deal. He deeply resented this. These would be two miserable and confusing hours that he would never see again. It would be like looking for Miss Walker's seed box all over again. Even if he did find a better deal, how would he know if the new insurer would be truly supportive if he ever made a claim? Things went from bad to worse because, even with the aid of various comparison websites, the two hours became four hours and confusion still reigned.

Brian was at the point of giving up. He had decided to ring Andrea to see what her plans were over the next few days and then, with Eve's usual precision timing, an email pinged in from across the Atlantic. It may have been the twenty-first century but Brian was always amazed by the speed of technology when there was not a wire in sight. He knew he was getting old. This had been rein-forced the day before when he had been in the early years foun-dation class and a youngster had been playing with a cardboard box model of a computer she had made. Brian dutifully praised the hard work that 4-year-old Sophie had put into her model and, in order to try to move on the learning, had said, 'When I was little I never played with a box model of a computer. Sophie, I wonder if you know why?' She looked up at Brian and said, 'Mr Smith, when you were a little boy they hadn't invented cardboard!' This was the point at which he had decided to go to the Year 6 classrooms instead and tell them off. He wasn't sure what to tell them off for but he was convinced he would think of something.

Brian looked at Eve's email:

Hi Bri,

Question: In the twenty-first century, institutions in which sector are the most resistant to change?

Answer: Education. And here's the proof: 80% of the time spent teaching mathematics is based around calculating by hand. That seems strange, especially as many of the teachers and children won't enjoy it and these days computers are actually very good at it. Mathematics has been liberated from calculating everywhere but in education.[1]

Why don't you become liberated and join me in the sun?

Eve x

Brian looked at the scribbled calculations relating to his home insurance policy. He was not enjoying the mathematics of being a consumer. If a relatively intelligent and well-educated person

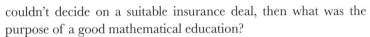

couldn't decide on a suitable insurance deal, then what was the purpose of a good mathematical education?

He made a note:

The real reasons to teach mathematics:

1. To allow people to fulfil the technical requirements of future employment (engineers, geologists, builders, astronauts, medical professionals, etc.).
2. To make appropriate decisions in everyday life including consumer issues and financial literacy.
3. To provide logical mind training.

Brian left the price comparison websites behind. They were depressing him anyway. His mind was now more focused on the teaching of mathematics. As he scrolled around the internet he found a significant calculation that had been performed by the mathematician Conrad Wolfram who argued that on one day, the equivalent of 106 average lifetimes is spent teaching children to calculate by hand.[2] To start with, Brian dismissed this as ridiculous as it was a Saturday, but then started to think that, if this really was the case, then we need to know why we are doing it, especially as it had offered little support to him in selecting a new home insurance policy. He jotted down:

Real mathematics is about posing the right questions that are based in the real world.

After that, it is about being able to accurately carry out the computation to find a solution to the problem.

Finally, it is about being able to work out if the question has been appropriately answered.

Brian knew that these were the principles by which he wanted to build a mathematics curriculum. He also knew there was a significant barrier and that was the testing regime which Rupert Brinton was now seeking to enhance further. If we test everybody by hand in mathematics, it will never aid curricular change to a point where we use computers to unleash the true power of mathematics. Brian was now deep in thought because he realised that the first country that did this would leapfrog all others in developing a new and improved economy. He went to the search engine on his computer once more to discover that Estonia had been named as the first country to implement an innovative computer based mathematics education programme, which suddenly reminded him that he hadn't rung Andrea to check out their weekend plans.

Bad news for Brian Smith

He dialled the number and waited. Andrea answered. He noticed the anxiety in her voice when she said, 'Brian, I can't make it to the Cotswolds!' Reasons for this were offered and Andrea really did sound upset. Brian suddenly felt devastated and, unfortunately, he failed to hear that.

There was a silence while he recovered his thoughts and in his disappointment mumbled, 'I guess there's no Father Christmas after all.' He couldn't really remember what Andrea said during the rest of the conversation. His mind had become numb. He was saddened by the news. This was the point at which he realised that his feelings for Andrea were stronger than he had imagined.

Bad news for Rupert Brinton

Brian wasn't the only one suffering bad news because there was further poor press for Rupert Brinton. In the 2016 budget, plans were drawn up to force all schools to be removed from local authority control to join a multi-academy trust. This was despite the fact that Ofsted had highlighted that the significant majority of primary schools were doing very nicely thank you. An outcry followed from educational professionals, governors, local councillors and even government backbenchers. The secretary of state for education demonstrated his resolve by saying there would be absolutely no reversing away from this plan.

It took less than two months for Rupert Brinton to hit the reverse gear and perform the twenty-fourth U-turn of the year for the government. The press accused him of failing to listen to advice and trying to bury the bad news around the time of local elections, and blamed him for creating a chaotic mess in schools.[3] The twenty-fifth U-turn came when the plans to test pupils on multiplication in 2017 were put on hold.

Chapter 17

Who wants to solve a quadratic equation anyway?

Primary school pupils should be taught about filling in tax returns and how to find the best mobile phone tariff, MPs insist

Daily Mail Online, 23 May 2016

'Now that's interesting,' thought Brian, 'a *Daily Mail* headline that seems sensible.' He knew it would be even more sensible had it included home insurance. He still hadn't resolved the issue of which insurer to place his business with; in fact, he had lost interest. Since Andrea had pulled out of the Cotswolds trip he had lost interest in many things, except Estonia. Indeed, he had even joked with Eve about meeting her by St Olaf's Church in Tallinn. More worryingly, he had even learned the many and varied translations of the Estonian national anthem. 'Can ever such a place be found, So well belov'd, from sense profound ...' goes one of the versions.

Brian considered that the notion of 'profound sense' had not always been easy to find in government policy in England. However, there was something refreshing about Estonian government policy relating to mathematics. As it was also Europe's top performing nation in the PISA rankings it could be considered to have delivered the results. Brian's research showed that teachers in Estonian schools have a high degree of autonomy about methodology, mixed ability teaching is the norm and teachers stay with their class for longer periods of time, thus allowing deeper relationships to develop, maintaining continuity and progression. As a consequence, the teachers are considered to be good at supporting students and preventing them going off track. Not only that, early years education is free, college education is free and even school lunches are free. As a result, children from even the most deprived backgrounds perform well. Brian couldn't help but wonder whether these policies would have an impact on the community that made up the super output area around Springett Lane.

Brian had also realised that the educators responsible for drawing up Estonia's approach to mathematics considered that too often the subject had been divorced from the real world. Therefore, there was a need to engage children in more difficult tasks based around using mathematics practically and for problem solving. Clearly there was a need for children to understand how to calculate accurately, but they also needed to understand the purpose of calculation without turning this into something they would start to hate. There reaches a point when competency in calculation is achieved when computers can take over anyway. This is what happens every day in the real world. Conrad Wolfram, the British entrepreneur behind the new Estonian national curriculum for mathematics, questions, for example, why we need to know the formula for solving a quadratic equation.[1]

Will it rain on 12 July?

It was on the day when Brian had found Daniel Taylor walking down the corridor with £150 in used £5 notes that his real interest in Estonia had been triggered. The money had indeed come from Rob Thirkettle who was the local butcher. However, unbeknown to Brian, in addition to running the shop around the corner, he also ran a range of other small businesses including a mobile hot potato oven that parked outside the town centre pubs at closing time every Friday and Saturday. Each winter he had a stall in the market selling Christmas trees, and best of all he had a vintage car which he hired out, complete with driver, for weddings. Rob was a successful businessman and he got a thrill out of it. Rob knew nothing about mathematics in Estonia and nobody would ever have regarded him as an academic. Nevertheless, he was a bit of a philosopher, and sometimes when the shop was quiet he would gaze over the estate which had helped make him wealthy and think, 'I ought to give something back to this community – something which might make a difference ...' He wanted to become the Springett Lane philanthropist.

In order to make a difference, Rob hatched a plan with a handful of other local business people and two of the teachers from the school to encourage the children to run their own mini-businesses. He thought this would raise aspiration and confidence and make them more employable in the future. The scheme would involve Rob loaning £5 to each child, who would then be required to be enterprising and entrepreneurial and set up their own business, with computerised published accounts, that would return a profit within one month. The profit would remain with the children and the £5 notes would be returned, interest free, to Rob. The children made smoothies, washed cars and made clocks out of CDs – they loved it. Some children went for it alone while others pooled their financial resources. The spirit of Justine Tyme and Estonian mathematics arrived at Springett Lane, courtesy of a man whose pork pies consistently won the blue ribbon of excellence.

While the project had been a great success, Brian knew that creating a different approach to teaching mathematics was going to be a complex process. The more he read and researched, the more Brian became pensive. He knew he had ideas and the next stage was to test them out, so he drew up a plan. He was going to go into the Year 6 class and say, 'I'm thinking of holding sports day on 12 July, but will it rain?' He would then step back and see what happened next. He knew the question seemed random but it was also part of an investigation quoted in the Estonian national curriculum for mathematics.

What happened next was high quality conversation, a checking of weather records, calculations of mean, median and mode averages and then turning decimal fractions into percentages in order to discover that 12 July would be a good day to hold sports day. Obviously, nobody could be certain of the weather, but the day dawned bright, the skies were blue and the clouds white and high. And that was the day Brian decided that mathematics was truly beautiful.

As the sack race came to an end, he reached for the notepad in his pocket:

The important elements of mathematics at Springett Lane:

* High quality calculation teaching.
* Seeking out patterns in numbers and mathematics.
* Enterprise education and financial literacy.
* Using computers and new technologies as regularly and appropriately as possible.
* Using mathematics across the whole curriculum.
* And, as it is sports day, let's make mathematics physical.

Arithmophobia

While Brian loved the principles of Estonian mathematics, he knew that it wasn't going to be easy to implement, but he really believed the journey would be worth it. He also knew he couldn't lead the innovation alone and he would need support. The issue of subject leadership was a thorny one. Across this nation there are many people who have negative feelings about mathematics. They don't immediately recognise its wonder or the creative opportunities it offers. Within Springett Lane, this issue was reflected across the staff team. The reality was that most teachers had a degree of competence in teaching calculation effectively, but Brian knew that dynamism needed to be injected and he was unsure how this could be achieved. He had thought about contacting Andrea but decided against it. He had not made any contact since she cancelled the Cotswolds trip. While he missed her, he thought it best to go it alone.

Meeting Andrea may have been out of the question, but Brian knew that Tom would say that sometimes it's the little things that help create transformational change. It was therefore time for another early morning coffee and to search for new butterflies.

Tom listened carefully to Brian as the coffee machine hissed into action, then he paused before stroking his stubbly chin – once again he had left the house too early to find time to shave. Brian, however, looked immaculate in his dark blue suit and well-ironed white shirt. After a second or two, Tom offered his considered butterfly saying, 'Currently there is much research into the area of mindsets,[2] but when it comes to mathematics there are too many people who simply have closed minds and believe they have an inherent weakness in the subject. Some people argue there is a condition called arithmophobia, which is a fear of numbers, and we don't do enough to fight it. Whenever we hear of people who reach adulthood with poor literacy skills, we consider it a tragedy that needs remedial action. But, too often, when the same is said about essential numeracy and calculation skills, we see folk shrug their shoulders and say "Me too!"'

Focus on the mindset

Tom's butterfly was to focus on creating growth mindsets and dispelling closed mindsets in mathematics. He went on to tell a powerful story about a school he had visited some twenty years previously, where a new young and vibrant head teacher called Paul had been appointed. The staff, who could best be described as dour, seriously challenged his enthusiasm. He told Tom that in staff meetings it was as though they sat with their arms folded and scowled at him. As the meeting closed, they would disappear into dark corners to discuss and dismiss the latest musings from their leader. They were trying to appear intelligent, knowledgeable and superior by heaping disparagement on Paul. They were afraid of trying new ideas because, if they failed, it would make them feel insecure. As a consequence, they had closed their minds to new ideas or simply disparaged anything they deemed too exciting. By the end of his first year, Paul had become totally ground down by the problem, but it was during the six week summer break that he hit upon his brainwave.

As the children arrived back after the summer holidays, they noticed that the sign saying 'head teacher' had been removed from his door and replaced with a new one: 'head learner'.[3] On that important first day of the school year, Paul walked into the assembly hall with a French horn under his arm. The children sat there wide eyed and somewhat worried as their leader announced that he was unsure which end he was supposed to blow. After much puffing and panting he managed to produce a sound. The more polite children simply described it as disgusting. The less polite ones compared it to a goose farting in the fog. He persevered

until eventually his face had turned the colour of a beetroot. At that point, he put down the instrument and said he knew it had sounded awful, but he would practise all year and then bring the instrument back on the last day of term and play the school hymn. Ten months later, to rapturous applause from the children, he not only fulfilled his pledge but succeeded with aplomb. The truth was that Paul had always harboured a desire to play a musical instrument but believed he would never be able to because he feared he couldn't read music. However, by changing his mindset he fulfilled a personal dream.

The next school year he challenged all the teachers to join him in mastering a new skill, while he would extend his new-found musical skills to learning the bagpipes. At first, staff resistance was high. But each night, as the staff left school, they could hear the wailing sound of the bagpipes and sometimes spotted Paul's purple face and bulging cheeks straining behind the instrument. As time went on, progress was made and through the use of accompanying CDs, the staff left to the faltering strains of 'Take Me Home, Country Roads', 'No Place Like Home' and even 'Homeward Bound'. Eventually those exceptionally long faces started to smile and even laugh, and some even joined in, singing the words. Paul didn't care whether they were laughing at him or about him. The truth was, they were laughing in school and they probably hadn't done that for years.

After a pause, Brian asked what happened next and Tom replied, 'The staff learned flower arranging, ballroom dancing and how to jump out of aeroplanes. Their mindset had changed from being closed to being open.'

Tom then suggested that Brian needed to appoint a subject leader for mathematics. This needed to be someone who might not be a natural or skilful mathematician but someone with an open mind and a can-do attitude. It needed to be someone who would cultivate mathematics across the whole curriculum in such a way that both children and staff would develop a growth mindset about the subject. It needed to be a subject leader who would promote the power, splendour and beauty of mathematics and not just the content of the national curriculum frameworks. This was essential because there is no doubt that in an information-driven world mathematics will be the mainstream subject of the future.

Brian wrote:

THE FIXED MINDSET
In order for some people to look 'smart' they tend to:

* Avoid new challenges.
* Give up easily when obstacles occur.
* See effort as fruitless or just lost time.
* Ignore feedback which could be helpful.
* Dumb down other people's successes because they feel threatened by them.

THE GROWTH MINDSET
As a result of a desire to learn and improve some people:

* Embrace challenges.
* Persist despite obstacles.
* See effort as a route to mastery.
* Learn from well-constructed criticism.
* Feel inspired by other people's success.

After Brian's fountain pen had been put away, Tom concluded his comments by referring to Andrea: 'Do you know, I have often wondered if you and Andrea should make a go of it. You seem ideally suited, but I suspect you never will because your own mind is closed and you fear rejection. Perhaps you should talk to her about mindsets. I bet she will have dozens of stories about successful people who had open minds.'

Brian explained why he was trying to keep his distance from Andrea and Tom told him he was crazy. Brian responded, 'Look, just because I talk to myself and collect *Daily Mail* headlines, it doesn't mean I'm going mad.'

'I was saying you were mad to avoid Andrea,' replied Tom. 'There is no problem with talking to yourself because at least you will know someone is listening. I always talk to myself when I need expert advice!'

'Was that last bit a butterfly?' asked Brian.

'It is certainly good advice,' replied Tom.

A touch of madness can go a long way

For once, Brian had been upset by Tom's remarks. He was still smarting from Andrea's rejection and he thought Tom would have been more understanding, but instead he accused him of being mad. While he was determined not to ring Andrea, he hadn't prepared himself for what he would do if Andrea phoned him, and that is precisely what happened next. His mobile phone vibrated and Andrea's name flashed across the screen. Partly through anxiety and partly through excitement, Brian showed his technological incompetence by pressing all the wrong buttons and taking yet another photograph of his foot. By the time he eventually got the phone to his ear he heard Andrea say, 'I have been thinking about you and madness.'

Initially, Brian wasn't sure what to say but he eventually managed to repeat his previous thoughts, although they were not necessarily coherent: 'I'm not going mad. I just talk to myself sometimes. Tom thinks I'm going mad too, but I'm not. Not only that, I think some of our best teachers may well be slightly crazy and there is nothing wrong with collecting *Daily Mail* headlines. Anyway, Andrea, what can I do for you?'

There was an uncomfortable silence until Andrea said, 'Can we start again? I was thinking about you and Madness? I have two tickets to see them – do you want to come with me? I wanted to apologise again for letting you down over the Cotswolds. I said I had a family problem, though I'm not sure you were listening. My sister was unwell and I had to spend the weekend looking after her children.'

Brian was pleased to hear the explanation. 'Madness?' he asked, feeling slightly foolish for thinking she was referring to his mental health.

'They are a band,' said Andrea.

'I know,' said Brian, 'I love them!'

Walt Disney, Abraham Lincoln and a bloke called Graham McPherson

Later that evening at their usual haunt, Brian started to tell the story of his morning's conversation with Tom on the issue of developing growth mindsets. Just as Tom had suggested, Andrea rattled off a string of famous people who had developed a remarkable growth mindset from a very low starting point. She jotted down some of the key points in Brian's notebook:

> Albert Einstein had very poor language skills until the age of 4 and his teachers believed this meant he would never amount to much. Maybe he demonstrated his growth mindset when he apparently said, 'Once we accept our limits, we can go beyond them.'
>
> Walt Disney was fired from his job as a journalist on a newspaper because he lacked imagination and had no original ideas.
>
> Abraham Lincoln, who is often deemed to be America's greatest president, failed in business, had a nervous breakdown and was defeated in eight elections before ridding the nation of slavery.

As Andrea stopped writing, she went on to say, 'Then, when it comes to schools, there is that hero of yours called Graham McPherson, whose school report said: 'McPherson seems incapable of understanding the simplest of procedures, questions or instructions. Together with the apparent lazy attitudes he exudes, it is therefore highly inevitable that he should obtain the above marks (Effort E, Attainment E). He is extremely slow and is, it seems, even incapable of copying a simple sentence from the blackboard. It goes without saying that any other form of work seems totally beyond him. I even wonder if I can hope for any sign of improvement.'[4]

Brian had no idea who Graham McPherson was but was appalled by the school report. He had always taken the view that these said more about the teacher than the child. Given Andrea's knowledge of highly successful people, Brian assumed that Graham McPherson was a successful businessman who had risen from rags to riches. In a way he was right, but he still needed to ask the question, 'Who is or was Graham McPherson, and what happened to him after he received that damning report?'

Andrea continued: 'The strange thing is, he made a fortune writing and then singing about all the fun he had at school learning "how to bend not break the rules". The song "Baggy Trousers" told his version of his schooldays and of the teachers who wrote his reports. Today the song remains so successful that he regards it as his pension.'[5]

After a pause Andrea added: 'In 2012, Graham McPherson – better known as Suggs, the lead singer of the band Madness – performed from the top of Buckingham Palace. By then he had sold millions of records and played in front of huge audiences. He is a published writer, actor, radio star and concert promoter and he raises funds for research to fight pancreatic cancer. All of this was achieved after a teacher described him as lazy and incapable of copying a simple sentence from a blackboard. This is surely a sign of the power of a growth mindset.'

Andrea told Brian that Tom was right and that he should look for a subject leader with an open mind who could promote mathematics to all children within a high belief, can-do culture.

After the third glass of wine Brian must have been feeling brave because he went on to tell Andrea that Tom said he had a closed mind about their friendship and Brian had told him quite categorically that they were just good friends. Andrea looked at Brian and, perhaps with a hint of disappointment, said, 'Well, yes, I guess so …'

The birth of beautiful mathematics

It would be fair to say that Margaret took some convincing before she agreed to take on the leadership of mathematics. The conversations between Brian and his new middle leader often felt more like complex diplomatic negotiations. Brian had recognised the qualities he was looking for. He saw in Margaret a sense of positivity and a desire to improve constantly as a professional and, because she was analytical in her practice, she would be able to articulate the importance of demonstrating and teaching growth mindsets in a mathematical context. The discussions were lengthy because Brian kept talking about his dreams for mathematics and developing a new style of teaching. He then left Margaret to ponder on whether she could fulfil the challenge and whether she wanted to fulfil the challenge. He often finished the conversations with the Art Williams quote, 'I'm not telling you it's going to be easy, I'm telling you it's going to be worth it.'

Commitment is what transforms a promise into reality

The first thing to say is that it continued to take time. To Brian it sometimes felt like too much time but Tom was always there urging patience. When progress was slow, he would turn to Brian and remind him: 'You have to reach that tipping point and you have to create those butterflies that will help you reach that tipping point. Eventually, with a mixture of inspiration, perspiration and downright resilience, you will arrive there. Then, when you have achieved the tipping point, it will be like watching one of those rallies where the dominoes fall one onto the other in sequence.' Andrea had also provided support for Brian to ensure he arrived at the tipping point, by reminding him of the work of Malcolm Gladwell.[6]

The three steps to reaching a tipping point:

1. Make your ideas contagious by constantly planting thoughts in the minds of others, when you judge that the time is right.
2. Remember that little causes have big effects.
3. Progress may be gradual but real change comes in one big dramatic moment.

Margaret started to grow steadily into the role and set up her classroom and the space around it as a 'hub of excellence for beautiful mathematics'. This was the title she was determined to give to the project. She had visited a number of other schools in the area to view their approaches to teaching and learning in the subject, and quickly realised that they were rapidly becoming interested in the work she was doing, allowing a form of mutual learning experience to take shape. Whoever said two heads were better than one was absolutely correct. Alicia Silverstone was even more correct when she wrote, 'Creative collaboration is awesome.'

Within the hub of excellence were attractive, interactive displays that drew the children in, and these were often based around 'could be' questions that provided a space for the children to respond. On other occasions 'would you rather' problems were set:

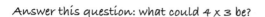

Answer this question: what could 4 x 3 be?

* The months of the year.
* Two boxes of eggs.
* A football team with one substitute.
* The first even number after 11.

Would you rather:

* Have 100 £1 coins?
* Win £1,800 and have to split it with 12 people?
* Have the savings from £1 invested 30 years ago, £2 invested 29 years ago or £3 invested 27 years ago?
* Have ten lottery tickets?

Elsewhere, there were displays of children's successful responses to maths investigations, practical resources and mathematical dictionaries. Each half term, Margaret led a celebration work assembly where children brought in samples of their successful learning in mathematics. Margaret used these opportunities to develop the language of growth mindsets, draw out patterns in mathematics and promote fun and dexterity. This gave her evidence of where the subject was being taught well, where good practice could be disseminated to others and where development work was needed.

However, there were two critical moments in Springett Lane's journey to reaching their tipping point for beautiful mathematics. As a result of her visits to other schools and the research she had carried out, it was decided that the mathematics curriculum should be divided into two.

First of all, it was absolutely essential that every class should be taught a high quality, high impact calculation lesson each day. The emphasis would be largely on direct teaching where teachers confidently imparted skills and knowledge in a style that was age appropriate and in a manner whereby they could see true relevance and purpose in the subject. In these lessons the children would develop a love of counting, calculating, looking for patterns in numbers and developing a rich mathematical vocabulary, using terms such as multiples, factor, digital root, prime number, square number and square root with confidence and joy. As and when their skills and knowledge developed towards a level of mastery, not only would they solve problems but they would also write poems of doubling and halving and stories involving addition, subtraction, percentages and fractions.

The second aspect was to ensure that elements such as data handling, space, shape, measure and probability were taught through the school's broader rich and diverse fourth-generation curriculum. Every opportunity to use the children's blossoming calculation skills would be planned for in the belief that added reality led to added impact. Within this aspect of the work, Brian and Margaret worked to ensure that the true spirit of Estonian mathematics was high profile in the classrooms at Springett Lane. Their intention was to make the children fully mathematically and financially literate through the use of mathematics in real-life situations that would equip them for a rapidly changing world.

Whether you think you can or you can't, you are probably right

It was late one night after school when Brian and Margaret were debating the progress that had been made so far that they started to extend their plans. Their conversation had returned to the issue of growth mindsets, and Brian was simply thinking out loud when he asked the question, 'Which group of people in life best demonstrate a growth mindset and how can we harness this in mathematics education?'

After a pause Margaret responded, 'It's the Rob Thirkettles – it's the entrepreneurs!' There was another pause as her mind began working overtime and she said, 'What if each year group works with a particular worthy charity over the course of the year to run a series of mini-businesses to raise much needed funds, while also finding out about the good works of that organisation?'

Brian was clearly impressed but never got a chance to speak because Margaret was now on a roll: 'One of the key elements of children running businesses is achieving value for money; therefore, we should also place an emphasis on children carrying out consumer tests. They could take responsibility for deciding which school uniform supplier offers the best value for money or which coach company we should use for a school visit. They could also examine a range of products within their own popular culture. By doing this, we can let calculation skills and new technologies work together to teach genuine financial literacy and equip the children for a more prosperous adult life.'

Brian looked up smiling and said, 'Margaret that is brilliant! Will it work?' Margaret responded with a mischievous grin and demonstrated her growth mindset by saying, 'We can make it work. Remember, great works are performed not by strength, but by perseverance.'

'Wow, did you think of that one?' asked Brian.

'No,' replied Margaret, 'you can attribute that one to Samuel Johnson. But I have been researching growth mindsets.'

'Welcome to the special group that the secretary of state calls "The Blob"!' said Brian.

The us and them schools

Brian may well have asked his Year 6 pupils whether it would rain on 12 July, but another good mathematical question might have been, 'If I work in a local authority school, how likely am I to make it on to the New Year's Honours list?' The broadsheet newspapers provided the answer and it was a resounding 'not very'. They accused Rupert Brinton and his government colleagues of bias for selecting those educationalists working in the private sector, multi-academy trusts or free schools to receive national recognition, thus labelling huge numbers of excellent, dedicated and hardworking teachers as second-class citizens. However, the problem didn't stop there. A real 'us and them' culture was developing that was far more serious. On the sixth anniversary of the government's education reforms, they were accused of widening the poverty gap by reinforcing existing patterns of social segregation and, in some cases, exacerbating them.[7]

Chapter 18
Without struggle there is no progress

Parents to keep pupils at home in 'strike' over tests: thousands may not attend classes in protest over tests taken by six and seven-year-olds

Daily Mail Online, 2 May 2016

Almost three years had passed since Brian made his decision to stand aloof from political intervention, and the moment of truth now beckoned. He had just replaced the handset following the initial telephone conversation with the lead inspector. The team from Ofsted would arrive with their clipboards in the morning. The die had been cast and it felt as though his fate now lay in the hands of others. Brian started to reflect on the journey that had got him here.

After a slow start, the concept of three-generational lessons within a fourth-generation curriculum had been well and truly embraced by the staff and children. At the outset, people didn't quite know how to respond and lots of conversations took place both formally and informally. In the early days Brian sometimes felt frustrated because, in terms of real change, the school was a centre of inactivity. However, after the first year the pace started to accelerate. The emergence of the hubs of excellence became a significant driving force. Brian had continued to get huge support from Andrea and Tom, and when his spirits were low Eve always managed to send an email that somehow reminded Brian that he was leading a twenty-first century school rather than one stuck in the past. The other great motivator and supporter became Anne Moody, who sometimes led from the front as she further developed the teaching of literacy through a rich, experiential and often outdoor curriculum. Sometimes she led from the middle by working in close collaboration with her colleagues and sometimes she led from the rear because she readily admitted to having certain gaps in her subject knowledge and expertise. The difference was that she was now far more open to her own personal development and had a strong desire to improve further. Nobody could now doubt her commitment to the Springett Lane cause.

While many successes had been celebrated along the journey, it had never been straightforward. Sometimes it felt as though it was three steps forward and two steps back. Those who have dared to be different will tell you of the moments of uncertainty they have had to overcome. Brian experienced low points and he remembered those occasions when his shoulders dropped and he found it difficult to look at himself in the mirror. There were many times when he preferred just to close his eyes and keep them closed. In those moments one of Tom's butterflies often provided him with the strength to move forward – a Sir Tim Brighouse quote that simply said, 'Our best leaders have optimism beyond bounds.'[1] Above the door in his room was another famous quotation: 'I am a slow walker but I never walk back,' to which Brian had added the words 'only forward'.

More recently, Brian got a boost from the head of Ofsted who, in a change of heart, seemed to be daring schools to be different. In his 2014 annual report he wrote the following, which Brian added to his notebook:

> Children should enjoy a curriculum that provides a rich variety of knowledge and experience in school, no matter what their skills and abilities, and regardless of their personal circumstances. For the past few years, the emphasis of Ofsted's inspection has rightly been on standards in English and mathematics. It is now time to broaden our focus ... it is vitally important that schools offer a broad and balanced curriculum that contributes to the social, moral, spiritual and cultural development of pupils. It is essential to prepare pupils for life in Britain today. In addition to reporting on the quality of schools' curricula in routine inspections, Ofsted will undertake a survey to identify the best examples of a broad and balanced curriculum in England this coming year.[2]

Brian had written down these words because he wanted Springett Lane to be one of the best examples of a broad and balanced curriculum. Similarly he copied the comments from the revised Ofsted inspection schedule of 2015 about outstanding schools:

> Staff reflect on and debate the way they teach. They feel deeply involved in their own professional development. Leaders have created a climate in which teachers are motivated and trusted to take risks and innovate in ways that are right for their pupils.[3]

All of the above had certainly become the norm at Springett Lane, but would Ofsted really want to give a clear mandate to such a school? By 7 p.m. Brian knew he could do no more. He put the final items into his briefcase, which had been a gift from Andrea. The thought of her gave him a warm glow, but this was immediately followed by anxiety as he wondered what she would think of him if the inspection went badly. He realised that, in a strange way, her opinions were more important to him than Ofsted's. It would be even worse if, all of a sudden, there was no purpose to their friendship. He knew that either situation would be devastating. Over the years, he had always taken positive steps to do the right thing at school and now he had created something magical. He decided it was time to take other positive steps that might help to create something else magical.

The final item into the briefcase was *The Guardian* and Brian glanced at the headline: 'Schools and the new parent power: this time, the fight is personal'.[4] Maybe the article captured the spirit of Brian's success. It also captured the mood of several articles in Britain's other broadsheets. By the middle of the second decade of the twenty-first century, there had been a series of teachers' strikes in protest at Rupert Brinton's educational policies. Things were deteriorating further for the secretary of state.

The paper reported on the rise of parent protest groups opposed to many of the government's key policies relating to education. Hands Off Our Schools Brighton and Hove had been successful in their campaign against forced academisation. The Anti Academies Alliance continued to highlight issues relating to the high salary payments and financial irregularities that existed in some academy chains. Rescue Our Schools raised concerns over the removal of the

requirement to have parent-governors in schools, behaviour policies and the curriculum. For Parents Defending Education, it was
almost a clean sweep across a wide range of issues such as spending
cuts, special educational needs, the growth of testing, mental health
issues and the narrowing of the curriculum. In May 2016, a small
but significant group of parents took strike action and kept their children off school in order to take part in fun family activities. Rupert
Brinton criticised them, arguing that they were seriously affecting
the education of their children. In May 2016, the *Daily Mail* questioned whether the strike was part of a wider political campaign
after they alleged there were possible ties with trade unions.[5] Perhaps
they should heed the wise words often attributed to Margaret Mead:
'Never doubt that a small group of thoughtful, committed citizens
can change the world. Indeed, it is the only thing that ever has.'

An end of term review might have concluded that surely things
had deteriorated even further. We had reached the stage where
there was a crisis of confidence at the Department for Education,
which was on a war footing and being run like a sitcom. There
were complaints about bullying being rife. Some parents accused
the secretary of state of having a breathtaking arrogance. Others
accused him of mixing business with pleasure. There was evidence
that government policies could lead to a generation of physically
and mentally unhealthy children. Potential bias had been identified in the inspection system in order to support specific government initiatives. New policies were preventing many children from
receiving an education whereby all their talents could be recognised
and developed, therefore they were not getting a rounded education. Messages coming from the Department for Education were
described as confusing and this was leading to a culture of fear and
uncertainty. Schools were facing a situation where tests were being
cancelled or abandoned. Vulnerable children were being exposed
to even greater risk, and now the parents and governing bodies were
starting to rise up against government policies.

Many people might have wondered if Rupert Brinton really
was a suitable person to be secretary of state for education. The
prime minister clearly thought he was. Brian didn't agree with
the government policies, and he demonstrated it by daring to be
different. His story is nearly complete.

Chapter 19
The power of being true to your beliefs

'Dear Father Xmas ... Please bring me some nice toys and a hymn book'

Daily Mail Online, 3 December 2015

A few weeks had passed since the hugely successful inspection and Brian and his new fiancée, Andrea, were chatting in their favourite spot. They were reflecting on Springett Lane's journey and how they would urge other school leaders to do the same. On their journey, they had learned that schools do what they are told to a satisfactory standard but they do what they believe in to an incredible standard.

However, there is a significant part of the story missing so let's rewind.

If you believe in magic you will live a magical life

You may well recall that back in one of Brian's darker moments, when he was struggling to bring about the transformational changes he sought for his school, Andrea had asked whether he believed in Father Christmas. Without a thought he had instantly replied, 'Of course not, do you?' Andrea had responded, 'Of course I do. If you are going to achieve the improbable you have to believe in the improbable.' Sadly he never heard her response because of the sound of the number 52 bus. Brian and Andrea had referred to the conversation various times over the subsequent years, but while Brian had admired the sentiment, he thought he would need a lot of hard evidence before he could believe there really was a Father Christmas.

Brian's confirmation of his existence came from the unlikely source of the *Daily Mail* as he read the story that was about to cure his bizarre obsession with their reporting. The story told of a 5-year-old girl who had 'posted' a letter to Father Christmas up a school chimney back in 1938. The letter came to light during building renovations. The story went on to confirm that Christine Churchill, who was now 82, had written the letter. She also confirmed that Father Christmas had indeed been good to her and that the toys and hymn book she had asked for duly arrived. The impact on Brian was twofold. First, he thought that finding a letter to Father Christmas in the school chimney could lead to a brilliant project in a fourth-generation curriculum at Springett Lane. Second, confirmation of the existence of Father Christmas had arrived.

As the post-inspection celebrations came to a conclusion (and every school should know how to celebrate its successes) and the school closed for the Christmas holidays, Brian presented Andrea with two plane tickets to Lapland. There they enjoyed sleigh rides and walks through pine forests before returning to their log cabin. The fire was burning brightly and providing a very warm glow. The cool champagne was helping to make Andrea feel very light-headed and Springett Lane seemed a million miles away. Suddenly the door of the log cabin blew open with an enormous bang. The wind howled and snowflakes blew in, and Father Christmas himself stood in the doorway bearing a small gift. Andrea turned to Brian who was now on one knee beside her, asking her if she would marry him and wear the ring that Father Christmas was offering to her.

When Andrea agreed, Brian turned to her and said, 'Then I believe in Father Christmas, because people who believe in magic will truly live a magical life.'

Endnotes

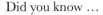

Did you know …

Preface
1   See Adam Vaughan, Boris Johnson accused of burying study linking pollution and deprived schools, and Jonathan Wolff, University research and the rise of academic bragging contests, both in *The Guardian* (17 May 2016).

Chapter 1: Begin with the end in mind
1   Over my career, I have had the privilege of working in many wonderful schools. As a consultant, I have worked in some of them on a more regular basis. The work in the text comes from St Alban's Catholic Primary School in Doncaster. The quote is from a recent school inspection report.
2   See Jonathan Smith, *The Learning Game: A Teacher's Inspirational Story* (London: Little, Brown, 2000), p. 70.
3   Another school I have worked in on a more regular basis is Woodthorpe Community Primary School in Sheffield, where the 'Grandpa Joe' work took place. It received an equally glowing inspection report.
4   I am indebted to the pupils and staff at St Bede's Catholic Primary School in Rotherham, with whom I have enjoyed a long working relationship. This extract comes from their inspection report.
5   The term 'nature-deficit disorder' was coined by Richard Louv in his book *Last Child in the Woods: Saving*

Our Children from Nature-Deficit Disorder (London: Atlantic Books, 2010).
6   Press Association, Government accused over 'chaotic' education policy after Bill dropped, *Daily Mail* (28 October 2016).

Chapter 2: A hero in waiting
1   The 2014/2015 report strongly praised England's primary schools for the quality of their work and the progress they were making. This was despite constant changes to the inspection framework that were designed to increase rigour. See Ofsted, *The Annual Report of Her Majesty's Chief Inspector of Education, Children's Services and Skills 2014/15: Education and Skills* which is available at: https://www.gov.uk/government/publications/ofsted-annual-report-201415-education-and-skills.
2   See Ofsted, *The Annual Report of Her Majesty's Chief Inspector of Education, Children's Services and Skills 2015/16: Education and Skills* which is available at: https://www.gov.uk/government/publications/ofsted-annual-report-201516-education-early-years-and-skills.
3   In an article in *The Times*, the former secretary of state for education, Michael Gove, described himself as a traditionalist, believing children learned best seated in rows, reciting poetry and learning the names of the kings and queens

of England. See A. Thomson and R. Sylvester, Gove unveils Tory plan for return to 'traditional' school lessons, *The Times* (6 March 2010). The phrase about teachers 'authoritatively imparting knowledge' in the classroom was written into Ofsted's definition of outstanding teaching reputedly on his instructions.

4　On 16 January 2012, Ofsted published a press release under the heading, Ofsted scraps 'satisfactory' judgement to help improve education. See https://www.gov. uk/government/news/ofsted-scraps-satisfactory-judgement-to-help-improve-education.

5　In 2012, despite huge cuts in government spending in an era of austerity, the then secretary of state, Michael Gove, promoted the building of a royal yacht costing around £60 million. He thought that schools could help to raise the cash. See P. Wintour, Give Queen a new royal yacht for diamond jubilee, says Michael Gove, *The Guardian* (15 January 2012). He also sent a bound King James Bible to all of England's schools. The cost was estimated at £370,000. Each bible had the inscription, 'presented by the secretary of state for education'. Michael Gove stated that philanthropists financially supported the scheme. See Press Association, Michael Gove defends £370,000 plan to send Bibles to schools, *The Guardian* (25 May 2012).

6　See Ofsted, *The Annual Report of Her Majesty's Chief Inspector of Education, Children's Services and Skills 2014/15*, p. 29. Behaviour in primary schools is a considerable strength and reflects well on all the professionals who work in them. The report adds: 'Of more than 16,000 primary schools, only 62 are currently judged inadequate for behaviour and safety.'

7　The annual Ipsos MORI Veracity Index in 2015 identified that just 25% of people trusted tabloid journalists to tell the truth. If teachers would like a further boost to their confidence, they were voted the second most trusted profession after doctors. See: https://www.ipsos. com/ipsos-mori/en-uk/politicians-are-still-trusted-less-estate-agents-journalists-and-bankers.

　　One of the reasons why journalists may seek to disparage state schools could be that a disproportionate number of them have received a public school education. The information in the text is adapted from Owen Jones, *The Establishment: And How They Get Away With It* (London: Allen Lane, 2014). Teachers should not necessarily believe all that tabloid newspapers say about education.

8　In January 2011, there were twelve Old Etonians in the government's inner circle. See F. Nelson, David Cameron's 'chumocracy' is no substitute for a political mission, *Daily Telegraph* (14 June 2012). Even cabinet member Michael Gove described it as preposterous. The satirical magazine *Private Eye* parodied David Cameron and his chums in the cartoon strip 'Dave Snooty and his New Pals'.

9　Many schools are brilliant at promoting themselves as exciting learning environments in a twenty-first century context. In contrast, Michael Gove reputedly placed a nineteenth century school desk in a key display area at the Department for Education.

10　Michael Gove frequently described educational researchers and academics (i.e. those who knew what they were talking about) as 'The Blob'. See, for example: I refuse to surrender to the Marxist teachers hell-bent on destroying our schools: education secretary berates 'the new enemies of promise' for opposing his plans, *Daily Mail* (23 March 2013).

11 If you want to dare to be different and like to display the occasional inspirational quote to help you along the way, then try the opening words of Bob Dylan's 'Gonna Change My Way of Thinking' from the 1979 album *Slow Train Coming*.

12 While Ofsted were reporting that the quality of leadership and management in primary schools was improving, there was evidence to suggest that this was not the case at the Department for Education. The MP and former education minister, Tim Loughton, accused Michael Gove of running the Department for Education like the TV sitcom, *Are You Being Served?* See, for example, M. Chorley, 'Terribly formal' Michael Gove accused of running education department like *Are You Being Served?* (by one of his own ministers), *Daily Mail* (16 January 2013).

Chapter 3: The sexy subversive

1 Many educational organisations that dare to be different and then pursue their ideals with rigour achieve fabulous success. For example, the considerable success of Rochdale Sixth Form College, which gained a judgement of outstanding, was reported on in: R. Garner, How Rochdale Sixth Form College taught its teens to think bigger, *The Independent* (5 June 2013).

2 In April 2013, James Dyson expressed his concerns about the secretary of state's vision for a more rigorous academic curriculum. He was especially concerned by the apparent relegation of design technology, arguing it was being diluted by puff pastry and topiary. He argued that the design technology curriculum should allow children to apply mathematical, scientific and technological knowledge to solve problems, rather than having thirty students making identical wooden key holders. See J. Dyson, Michael Gove overlooks engineering at his peril, *The Guardian* (15 April 2013).

3 See L. Woodhead, *Shopping, Seduction & Mr Selfridge* (London: Profile Books, 2007), p. 36. The book tells the remarkable leadership story of Harry Gordon Selfridge and how, through a vision of the future and what the best might look like, he changed shopping in the United Kingdom forever.

4 Ibid., p. 36.

5 Ibid., p. 32.

6 Secretaries of state for education have often disparaged educationalists and even sought to belittle them. Sir Tim Brighouse once sued a previous education secretary, John Patten, for calling him a 'madman' who went around 'frightening the children'. Sir Tim Brighouse used some of the money to set up the University of the First Age. See J. Judd, Patten offers education chief a libel settlement, *The Independent* (23 May 1994).

7 In leadership, little acts can make a huge difference. This is sometimes referred to as the 'butterfly effect'. For more on this see Sir Tim Brighouse and David Woods, *Inspirations: A Collection of Commentaries and Quotations to Promote School Improvement* (London: Network Continuum Education, 2006).

8 Not only did the evidence suggest

that politicians frequently failed to tell the truth as indicated in the annual Ipsos MORI Veracity Index, but a disproportionate number of them also failed to obey the law. In 2011, *Private Eye* (edition 1289) stated that 0.13% of the general population was in prison as compared with 0.61% of MPs from the last parliament who were in prison.

9   Department of Education and Science, *Primary Education: Suggestions for the Consideration of Teachers and Others Concerned with the Work of Primary Schools* (London: HMSO, 1959).

10   See http://news.bbc. co.uk/onthisday/hi/ dates/stories/october/9/ newsid_3095000/3095531.stm.

11   Department of Education and Science, *Primary Education*, p. 113.

12   Ibid., p. 78. Despite common perceptions, there were many enlightened and forward thinking schools around in the 1950s. The principles that underpinned many of these establishments are still relevant today.

13   Quoted in J. Bernstein, *Albert Einstein and the Frontiers of Physics* (New York: Oxford University Press, 1996), p. 32.

14   This extract comes from the surprisingly more enlightened era of 1935. It was published by the Board of Education in the *Handbook of Suggestions for Teachers*, p. 309.

15   See the Audit Commission's *Value for Money in Schools – Literature and Data Review. Final Report*, published in March 2008, which indicated that schools were among the most respected organisations in a local community.

16   In March 2013, *The Times* and *The Guardian* published articles about students deserting arts subjects at GCSE because of the then secretary of state's 'hokey cokey' approach towards them. One minute they were in and the next they were out of his proposed educational baccalaureate. See, for example, G. Hurst, Pupils deserting arts subjects at GCSE 'because of Gove reforms', *The Times* (25 March 2013).

Chapter 4: Every time I use my mobile I take a photograph of my foot

1   Albert Einstein uttered this famous quote during an interview conducted by George Sylvester Viereck for the *Saturday Evening Post* in 1929.

2   During an interview with BBC Radio 4's *Today* programme in 2011, Michael Gove stated that there was too great a focus on teaching styles and not enough emphasis on teaching facts to young people. See Gove stresses 'facts' in school curriculum revamp (20 January 2011).

3   During the redrafting of the national curriculum in 2013, the then secretary of state, Michael Gove, said there should be an increased emphasis on teaching the nation's glorious past. He especially wanted to see a focus on teaching the British Empire.

4   In Charles Dickens' book, *Hard Times*, the schoolmaster, Thomas Gradgrind, famously said, 'Now, what I want is, Facts. Teach these boys and girls nothing but Facts. Facts alone are wanted in life. Plant nothing else, and root out everything else. You can only form the minds of reasoning animals upon Facts: nothing else will ever be of any service to them. This is the principle on which I bring up my own children, and this is the principle on which I bring up these children.

Stick to Facts, sir!' However, from this strong position even Gradgrind realises that this will eventually do damage and goes on to say: 'The ground on which I stand has ceased to be solid under my feet.' His own children's problems teach him to feel love and sorrow, and Gradgrind becomes a wiser and humbler man, ultimately 'making his facts and figures subservient to Faith, Hope and Charity'.

5   The French national curriculum, which was rewritten in 2012, places a strong emphasis on teaching right from wrong and what is fair and unfair.

6   Writing a letter to his younger self as he turned seventy, Paul McCartney reflected on the dreams he had as a teenager. These included fantasies of being successful in life as well as dreams of what a better world might look like. See P. McCartney, John and I had a premonition of success, *Big Issue* (16 February 2012).

7   State education arrived in England in the Victorian era and is still largely organised on the same principles. It has not kept pace with modern technologies, reducing the capacity of children to think creatively, and their ability to change is thwarted by a constant emphasis on testing. These are the key messages in the short film 'Changing Education Paradigms' by Sir Ken Robinson. It can be found at: https://www.ted.com/talks/ken_robinson_changing_education_paradigms.

8   Professor Robin Alexander is a highly significant writer and researcher in the world of primary education. As part of a review led by Cambridge University, he highlighted what a high quality primary education might look like in the book, *Children, Their World, Their Education* (Abingdon and New York: Routledge, 2009). However, like others, he recognised that too often primary education is drawn backwards rather than moving forwards. The quote in the text confirms this. It is taken from *Culture and Pedagogy: International Comparisons in Primary Education* (Malden, MA: Wiley-Blackwell, 2001), p. 39.

9   Leonard Marsh was a highly regarded writer and speaker in the world of primary education. He went on to become principal of Bishop Grosseteste University in Lincoln. He was a fervent believer in high quality experiential learning. The quotation used is taken from *Alongside the Child: Experiences in the Primary School* (London: A&C Black, 1970), p. 53.

10 In *Joys and Sorrows: Reflections* (New York: Simon & Schuster, 1970), Pablo Casals stresses the importance of teachers opening children's eyes to the beauty that is all around them, rather than merely imparting facts. The quote appears in Brighouse and Woods' volume, *Inspirations*, p. 131.

11 This quote is often accredited to Anthony Tasgall.

12 A report, jointly commissioned by the Association of School and College Leaders and the National Education Trust, indicated that young people spent the equivalent of a year preparing for or sitting examinations. The report also stated that the examination system had narrowed the curriculum and diminished the value of the education system. The report was published in January 2010 and reported in G. Paton, School pupils 'spend a year taking exams', *Daily Telegraph* (6 January 2010).

13 In a speech at the 'Collaborate,

Create and Educate' conference, at the Barbican in London on 3 June 2003, the then secretary of state for education, Charles Clarke, stressed the importance of high quality creativity and children having a rich and enjoyable childhood. He told school leaders that enjoyment was the birth right of every child. Teachers should never forget this message. Many regarded this speech as signposting the coming of the 'Excellence and Enjoyment' programme which was launched as part of the Primary National Strategy.

14 Department for Education and Skills, *Excellence and Enjoyment: A Strategy for Primary Schools* (Norwich: DfES, 2003).

15 Department for Children, Schools and Families, *Independent Review of the Primary Curriculum: Final Report* [Rose Review] (Nottingham: DCSF, 2008).

16 In 2005, Ofsted carried out a review into the impact of the Primary National Strategy across 47 local authorities. They concluded that 'very little had been done by schools to take greater responsibility for changing the curriculum' and the underlying reason was fear of a fall in the outcomes of statutory assessments, or criticisms from Ofsted inspectors or the local authority. This sense of fear was debilitating to schools but, alas, little has been done to improve the situation. The *Primary National Strategy: An Evaluation of its Impact in Primary Schools 2004/05* is available on the Digital Education Resource Archive website: http://dera.ioe. ac.uk.

17 This is a much used quotation but who actually said it first is unclear. Among those to whom it has been attributed are Mary Kay Ash,

Casey Strengel, Steve Backley, Tommy Lasorda, Jim Lovell or you could just go with 'anonymous'.

18 In May 2005, the Labour government recognised the importance of teaching children about the social and emotional aspects of learning, thus recognising that equipping children to overcome barriers and develop resilience were important in the learning process. In May 2005, the Department for Education and Skills published *Excellence and Enjoyment: Social and Emotional Aspects of Learning*.

19 During the first decade of the twenty-first century, many schools placed an emphasis on children's preferred learning styles (visual, auditory and kinaesthetic) as promoted by Neil Fleming and David Baume in Learning styles again: VARKing up the right tree! *Educational Developments*, 7 (2006), 4–7.

20 Guy Claxton argued in his book, *Building Learning Power: Helping Young People to Become Better Learners* (Bristol: TLO Ltd, 2002), that the key to successful learning lay in unlocking learning behaviours, building learning habits and developing a powerful learning character.

21 Howard Gardner suggested that an individual could be intelligent in a number of ways and that it was the duty of educators to recognise this and promote it. See *Frames of Mind: The Theory of Multiple Intelligences* (London: Heinemann, 1983).

22 Arthur Costa's work based on developing Habits of Mind was adopted by many schools in the period between 2000 and 2010. They believed that this focus enabled children to learn and retain skills and knowledge effectively. See *Developing Minds: A Resource Book for Teaching Thinking*

(Alexandria, VA: Association for Supervision & Curriculum Development, 2001).

23 Following huge concerns about the state of primary education and the impact of centrally imposed initiatives, Professor Robin Alexander was commissioned by the University of Cambridge to carry out a major review. See *Children, Their World, Their Education* (2009).

24 The Cambridge Primary Review was not the only significant review of the primary curriculum carried out in the first decade of the twenty-first century. The then Labour government also carried out a significant review into the state of the English national curriculum, headed by Sir Jim Rose, which led to the publication of a new national curriculum. This was based on huge amounts of research but was promptly scrapped by the new coalition government in 2010. The research can be found in the *Independent Review of the Primary Curriculum: Final Report* [Rose Review] published by the Department for Children, Schools and Families in 2008.

25 Bob Marley said, 'We don't have education, we have inspiration; if I was educated I would be a damn fool,' in a 1992 documentary about his life story, *Time Will Tell*, directed by Declan Lowney.

26 In September 2013, *The Independent* reported that there was a crisis of confidence at the Department for Education and that bullying was rife. See R. Garner, Crisis of confidence among civil servants in Gove's department, *The Independent* (23 September 2013). The account was based on a report produced by the National Audit Office.

Chapter 5: Wanted: invisible leaders – apply here

1 Oh, whatever happened to the long game? The first thing that happens in leadership is that you stop the clock and think about what your organisation will become in the future. There is much evidence to suggest that many UK organisations are over-managed and under-led. The extract in the text comes from *What Leaders Really Do* by John P. Kotter (Boston, MA: Harvard Business School Press, 1999), p. 13.

2 Jim Collins took the debate on leadership versus management further by defining the key qualities of what he calls 'Level 5 leaders'. These should be significant traits for all who lead any organisation. He did this in his book *Good to Great* (London: Random House, 2001), p. 93.

3 Steve Jobs, the founder of Apple, argued that there is a tendency in leadership to over-complicate things when simplicity is often the best approach. He frequently commented that the art of truly focusing was about saying no rather than yes. The information in the text is taken from Alastair Campbell's book, *Winners and How They Succeed* (London: Arrow, 2015), p. 16.

4 On 30 April 1939, when the New York World's Fair opened, the *New York Times* predicted a bleak future for television. On 12 February 2012, *The Independent* published an article by Brian Viner entitled 'The man who rejected the Beatles'. In 2008, Robert Strohmeyer stated that Tom Watson's prediction that the world would only ever need five computers was the most foolish ever. See R. Strohmeyer, The 7 worst tech predictions of all time, *PCWorld* (31 December 2008).

5 In July 2012, *The Times, The Guardian* and *The Independent* all

covered stories about the then secretary for state enjoying a holiday in Marrakech with a well-known celebrity chef. On their return to the UK, Michael Gove promptly named Henry Dimbleby the Department for Education's school meals adviser. See, for example, J. Merrick, Gove and Leon chef dreamed up school meals deal over mojitos in Marrakech, *The Independent* (15 July 2012).

Chapter 6: Books, not bullets, will change the world

1 The books and research of Guy Claxton have regularly promoted the importance of learning to learn. A powerful example of this is *Learning to Learn – The Fourth Generation: Making Sense of Personalised Learning* (Bristol: TLO Ltd, 2006).

2 In April 2012, both *The Guardian* and the *Daily Telegraph* covered articles in which celebrity TV chef Jamie Oliver criticised Michael Gove for lowering the standards of school meals. Oliver is quoted as saying, 'We don't want bullshit about the big society. We want a strategy to stop Britain being the fifth most unhealthy country in the world and the most unhealthy country in Europe.' See, for example, T. Helm, Jamie Oliver in blistering attack on Michael Gove over poor school diet, *The Guardian* (22 April 2012).

Chapter 7: People who moan about people who moan

1 In May 2012, Her Majesty's Chief Inspector of Schools launched a stinging attack on teachers saying that they don't know what real pressure is. His comments were made to a conference for independent school leaders in Brighton. See J. Shepherd,

Teachers don't know what stress is, says Ofsted chief, *The Guardian* (10 May 2012). By contrast, a Department for Education survey revealed that secondary heads worked an average of 63.3 hours per week; the longest of any of the teaching jobs. Primary classroom teachers worked longer hours at 59.3 than their secondary school counterparts, who worked 55.7 hours a week. The hours in a secondary academy were slightly less, at 55.2 hours. See J. Higton, S. Leonardi, N. Richards, A. Choudhoury, N. Sofroniou and D. Owen, *Teacher Workload Survey 2016. Research Report* (February). (London: Department for Education, 2017).

2 See H. Stewart, *The Happy Manifesto: Make Your Organization a Great Workplace* (London: Kogan Page, 2013), p. 136.

3 Stewart's *The Happy Manifesto* was written around these principles: try to imagine a workplace where people are energised and motivated by being in control of their workload. Imagine they are trusted and given freedom, within clear guidelines, to decide how to achieve their results.

4 In my first book I wrote about 'inside out leadership' – *Leadership with a Moral Purpose: Turning Your School Inside Out* (Carmarthen: Independent Thinking Press, 2008). Nelson Mandela could be described as the archetypal inside out leader. He knew what the community needed and he had a clear set of values in his mind, heart and soul. The film *Invictus* (2009), which covers events in South Africa around the 1995 Rugby World Cup shortly after the dismantling of apartheid, captures this spirit. It should be recommended viewing on leadership courses.

5   On 4 November 2012, *The Independent* published an article describing how Michael Gove had overruled many bodies and agreed to the selling off of school playing fields. See M. Calvin, The last word: Gove is selling children short; see also J. Adetunji, Michael Gove overruled experts to sell school playing fields, *The Guardian* (17 August 2012). On 13 December 2013, C. Hope, writing in the *Daily Telegraph*, claimed that a school field was being sold every three weeks, according to government figures.

Chapter 8: Six $1.5 million words

1   In April 2013, Nevada's tourism officials launched a new campaign to promote their state. See R. N. Velotta, A six-word slogan, and the marketing campaign to advertise it, cost Nevada $9 million, *Las Vegas Sun* (9 April 2013).

2   James Hilton's novel *Goodbye, Mr Chips* (London: Hodder & Stoughton, 1934) tells the story of a public school teacher who uses many strategies that the traditionalist might question, including promoting outdoor learning.

3   In May 2016, the *Daily Telegraph* reported on Chris Packham's comments at the Hay Festival where he was speaking about his memoir, *Fingers in the Sparkle Jar* (London: Ebury, 2016). See P. Foster, Chris Packham: eat tadpoles to learn value of animal life, *Daily Telegraph* (29 May 2016).

4   In 2005, Dr Richard Louv wrote a book called *Last Child in the Woods* which promotes the importance of children spending time outdoors. He also campaigns to prevent children suffering from nature-deficit disorder. The extract is based on this book.

5   In April 2014, the nation's newspapers had a field day (so to speak) when they reported that Northumbria Police had rounded up a small group of girls for developing their den building skills in local woods. The police later admitted that their actions had been over the top. See, for example, L. Brown, Parents' fury after young girls who built den during holidays moved on by police who checked if they had Asbos, *Daily Mail* (21 April 2014).

6   In his book *Last Child in the Woods*, Dr Richard Louv, citing James Clark (professor of kinesiology at the University of Maryland) and research from the University of Glasgow, argues that children are increasingly inactive. He states that some toddlers in the sample were only active for twenty minutes a day.

7   There have often been misconceptions about what inspectors are looking for during an Ofsted inspection and this causes teachers to 'play safe'. For example, Ofsted have reported on the significance of outdoor learning across all phases and key stages, stressing that memorable experiences lead to memorable learning. The example is taken from Ofsted's *Learning Outside the Classroom: How Far Should You Go?* (2008).

8   In November 2012, the *TES* reported that playtimes were dying a slow death as a result of a target led educational system. See H. Ward, All work and no play, *TES* (2 November 2012). The same thing was happening in the United States. When playtime, or recess as it is known there, was banned in Atlanta's public schools in the late 1990s, Benjamin O. Canada,

then the superintendent of public schools in Atlanta, told the *New York Times*: 'We are intent on improving academic performance. You don't do that by having kids hanging on the monkey bars.' See D. Johnson, Many schools putting an end to child's play, *New York Times* (7 April 2008).

9   In April 2013, the *TES* published an article on the lack of background information available about Ofsted inspectors. It claimed that Ofsted had been accused of failing to fulfil its promise to be 'open and transparent' about the backgrounds of its inspectors, prompting concerns from heads that schools were being given the wrong ratings by inexperienced staff. In an embarrassing series of revelations, Ofsted was forced to admit that it did not hold simple information about its inspectors' teaching experience. One of the private firms it had been using admitted that some of its inspectors did not have even basic teaching qualifications. See W. Stewart, Ofsted faces legal action from inspectors, *TES* (5 April 2013).

10 In August 2014, *The Observer* published an article which alleged that certain academy chains knew the dates of Ofsted inspections in advance. See W. Mansell and D. Boffey, Academies run by 'superhead' received advance notice of Ofsted checks, *The Independent* (17 August 2014).

Chapter 9: The three signs of a miserable job

1   Patrick Lencioni wrote a highly recommended book called *The Three Signs of a Miserable Job: A Fable for Managers (and their Employees)* (San Francisco, CA: Jossey-Bass, 2007). He argued that there were three

contributing factors to a lack of job satisfaction:

- Anonymity because you are basically doing a job the same way as everybody else does it. (Recent governments have been accused of a 'one size fits all' model of teaching.)
- Irrelevance because you may not even think you are doing the right thing. (Many argue that there was a clear lack of consultation in the implementation of the national curriculum, with many of those responsible for producing the documentation resigning.)
- Immeasurability because you feel you are not measuring the right things. (England's schools continue to be the most tested schools in the western hemisphere, with a simplistic emphasis on academic standards in literacy and numeracy.)

2   In *The Tipping Point* (London: Abacus Books, 2002), Malcolm Gladwell argues that most new initiatives are often greeted with resentment, but through skilled leadership and management strategies more and more people come on board until a tipping point is achieved and the initiative becomes fully embraced.

3   In November 2011, the coalition government launched a National Plan for Music. Strangely, it recommended that local authorities should stop funding music tuition. Many thought that this would simply leave music as the preserve of the middle classes. It also angered many musicians, including the internationally renowned cellist Julian Lloyd Webber. See W. Mansell, Free schools fail Ofsted inspections at much higher rate than state schools, *The Guardian* (29 April 2014).

Chapter 10: When teachers learn from each other, their future will be secured

1   In February 2016, Her Majesty's Chief Inspector of Schools, Michael Wilshaw, stated in his monthly commentary that teachers were now flocking abroad and the country was facing a 'teacher brain drain'. He calculated that in 2014/2015 an estimated 100,000 full time teachers from the UK were working in the international sector, 'making us the world's biggest exporter of teaching talent'. See: https://www.gov.uk/government/speeches/hmcis-monthly-commentary-february-2016.

2   The educationalist Michael Fullan has long advocated key strategies for school improvement based around collaboration and teachers learning from each other within a partnership of equals. The quotation in the text is taken from *Leading a Culture of Change* (San Francisco, CA: Jossey-Bass, 2001), p. 92.

3   During the 2014/2015 academic year, the then secretary of state for education, Nicky Morgan, frequently criticised coasting schools. She was eventually encouraged to provide a definition for the term. On 30 June 2015, she finally did so on BBC Radio 4's *Today* show. Comments on the programme's website indicated that many found the definition confusing.

Chapter 11: The problem with fronted adverbial clauses

1   I am indebted to the brilliant young writers at St Bede's Catholic Primary School in Rotherham for their contributions.

2   In August 2010, a survey of 2,000 children for the television channel Eden indicated that many young people thought that cows hibernate in winter. The report expressed concerns about the amount of time youngsters were spending outdoors. See J. Henley, Why our children need to get outside and engage with nature, *The Guardian* (16 August 2010).

3   In 2016, the Canal and River Trust carried out a survey which revealed there was a significant generation gap in the aspects of nature today's children could identify, compared with their parents and grandparents. Surveying toddlers to OAPs, the results showed that 25% of parents and 30% of children could not identify the sound a duck makes. As a consequence, they commented, 'This year we're calling on everyone to "Stop, Look and Listen" to what's happening around them, following our own survey results, which show surprising gaps in people's nature knowledge.' Materials were provided for families to support this work. See: https://canalrivertrust.org.uk/news-and-views/news/generational-gap-in-nature-knowledge-revealed.

4   In 2004, the Primary National Strategy produced a pack of professional development materials to support high quality primary teaching. It included a video recording entitled 'Earthwatch: Learning and Teaching in the Outdoors' which promoted the importance of high quality experiential learning outdoors. The materials were published by the Department for Education and Skills as *Excellence and Enjoyment: Learning and Teaching in the Primary Years* in 2004.

5   A survey by the charity Young Minds, published in January 2014, found a huge rise in issues relating

to the mental health and well-being of young people. Newspapers such as *The Times*, *The Guardian* and *The Independent* examined the role government policy and austerity cuts had played in this rise. See, for example, Press Association, Children's mental health menaced by 'unprecedented toxic climate', *The Guardian* (20 January 2014).

6   On 1 November 2013, *The Guardian* reported on how the government intended to remove coursework from GCSE examinations: see H. Muir, Michael Gove's new GCSE exams leave pupils without a second chance.

Chapter 12: This is the kind of English up with which I will not put

1   England's first spelling, punctuation and grammar test was introduced in May 2013. The confused cyclist example was one of the questions.

2   The English language is something beautiful and is not to be regarded as a test, but too often it is brought back to that level. The information used comes from the introduction to *English for Natives: Discover the Grammar You Don't Know You Know* by Harry Ritchie (London: John Murray, 2013), p. 1.

3   The last significant national review of how we teach English in our schools was *A Language for Life* [the Bullock Report] in 1974. It sought to provide young people with the oracy, reading and writing skills that would allow them to live fulfilled lives. After some initial impact, it has been largely forgotten, especially by education ministers who believe they know better.

4   *The Idler* magazine is a quarterly publication, possibly aimed at those with too much time on their hands. In 2013 they published their inaugural 'Bad Grammar' awards, and a key contender was an open letter written by 100 academics criticising Michael Gove for eroding educational standards. It was judged to be 'simply illiterate', with particular censure heaped on the sentence: 'Much of it demands too much too young.' See A. Flood, Academics chastised for bad grammar in letter attacking Michael Gove, *The Guardian* (3 May 2013). However, for every grammarian who was appalled by it, another argued that it was perfectly correct. Regardless of their opinions, I think we all know what it means.

5   George Bernard Shaw frequently railed against the 'taboo of grammar pedants'. He described one of them using phrases such as ignoramus, idiot and self-advertising duffer. The extract in the text comes from a letter to *The Times* in 1907.

6   Lord Bew was commissioned to report on assessment and accountability, the 2011 *Independent Review of Key Stage 2 Testing, Assessment and Accountability*. The interim and final report made no reference to the need for a spelling, grammar and punctuation test. The report was well referenced. Then, tagged on at the end, came a recommendation that there should be such a test because the answers could only be right or wrong. There was no rigorous cross-referencing in this section. You can find the report at: https://www.gov.uk/government/publications/independent-review-of-key-stage-2-testing-assessment-and-accountability-final-report.

7   In February 2014, the then secretary of state for education, Michael Gove, urged schools to punish badly behaved children by getting them to write lines.

This is a strategy that would do little to promote a love of writing. Most newspapers covered this story including *The Guardian*: Michael Gove urges 'traditional' punishments for school misbehaviour (2 February 2014).

8   *A Language for Life* (1975) was especially critical of teachers giving children decontextualised grammar and punctuation exercises, suggesting they would do little to improve the quality of children's writing. The quote appears on p. 171.

9   Similar comments and concerns about grammar and punctuation were made in an earlier review, in 1921, by the Departmental Committee of the Board of Education in *The Teaching of English in England* [Newbolt Report]. The quote in the text appears on p. 72.

10 If ever a piece of writing conjured up the magic of the English language, it is 'I Like Words'. It was written in 1934 by Robert Pirosh and appears in Shaun Usher, *Letters of Note: Correspondence Deserving of a Wider Audience* (London: Canongate, 2013), p. 36.

11 Simon Sinek promotes an inspirational model of leadership in his 2009 TED Talk, 'How Great Leaders Inspire Action'. He argues that too few leaders can answer the big question of 'why?' He quotes the work of those who could answer this question. They include the founders of Apple, Martin Luther King and the Wright brothers. His talk can be found at: https://www.ted.com/talks/simon_sinek_how_great_leaders_inspire_action.

12 In May 2014, many academics reacted angrily to Michael Gove's insistence that certain books be dropped from the GCSE curriculum. These included numerous award-winning texts that examined a range of significant issues. The subject was covered by many newspapers, including *The Guardian* on 25 May 2014: M. Kennedy, *To Kill a Mockingbird* and *Of Mice and Men* axed as Gove orders more Brit lit. The quote is a tweet by the actor Mark Gatiss.

13 Evidence from the Progress in International Reading Literacy Study (PIRLS) in 2006 indicated that reading for pleasure outweighed every social advantage including the parents' income in determining later success. See I. V. S. Mullis, M. O. Martin, A. M. Kennedy and P. Foy, *PIRLS 2006 International Report: IEA's Progress in International Reading Literacy Study in Primary Schools in 40 Countries* (Chestnut Hill, MA: TIMSS & PIRLS International Study Centre). The information was reported in *The Independent* on 6 December 2007.

Chapter 13: Three-generational lessons within a fourth-generation curriculum

1   Carmine Gallo's *Talk Like TED: The 9 Public-Speaking Secrets of the World's Top Minds* (New York: St Martin's Press, 2014) analyses the public speaking secrets of those who have had huge viewings for their online TED Talks. Teachers could learn a great deal about their own delivery from this book.

2   Andrew Stanton, the writer of the film *Toy Story*, presented a TED Talk in 2012 in which he stated, 'We all love stories; we were born for them.' See: https://www.ted.com/talks/andrew_stanton_the_clues_to_a_great_story.

3   In April 2016, the media announced that the government were planning to scrap controversial tests which

were to be administered in the early years foundation stage. Many educationalists had already advised that they would prove to be an unreliable and costly error. See, for example, J. Gurney-Read, 'Unfair' primary school baseline assessments dropped as progress measure, *Daily Telegraph* (8 April 2016).

Chapter 14: Leopards, peanuts and compost tip Brian over the hedge

1 In order to promote the wonderful and diverse talents of young people in the United Kingdom, professors David Winkley and Sir Tim Brighouse set up the Children's University. David Winkley was also a director of the National Primary Trust. The comments quoted were made at the National Primary Trust's annual conference at Aston University in 2001.

2 This quote is by Vera Nazarian and comes from *The Perpetual Calendar of Inspiration: Old Wisdom for a New World* (Highgate Center, VT: Norilana Books, 2010), p. 451.

3 A survey into pupils' attitudes to reading in the period after the implementation of the National Literacy Strategy showed that fewer children were now enjoying reading books. See M. Sainsbury and R. Clarkson, *Attitudes to Reading at Ages Nine and Eleven: Full Report* (Slough: National Foundation for Educational Research, 2008). Available at: https://www.nfer.ac.uk/publications/RAQ01.

4 As early as 1921, *The Teaching of English in England* [Newbolt Report] spoke of the dangers of teaching reading in a mechanical way that didn't promote a curiosity in books.

5 The Organisation for Economic Co-operation and Development analysed the outcomes of PISA tests relating to reading and concluded that reading for pleasure had a significant impact on a child's future life chances. The report was entitled *Reading for Change: Performance and Engagement Across Countries* and was published in 2002.

6 In 2013, the National Literacy Trust reported that children and young people are reading less and are now more likely to feel embarrassed if they are caught reading. They argued that this was detrimental as those who enjoyed reading outperformed age related expectations. The outcomes were reported in Christina Clark's *Children's and Young People's Reading in 2012: Findings from the 2012 National Literacy Trust's Annual Survey*.

7 In 2005, the National Literacy Trust also expressed concerns about the fact that fewer people chose to read. Christina Clark and Amelia Foster's report was called *Children's and Young People's Reading Habits and Preferences: The Who, What, Why, Where and When*.

8 In 2009, Ofsted reported that schools were not doing enough to encourage young people to read for pleasure. Their evidence was published in *English at the Crossroads* and was based on visits to 122 primary schools and 120 secondary schools between 2005 and 2008. Commenting at the time, the children's laureate Anthony Browne said: 'if children are not encouraged to read for pure pleasure, if they are dragged away from reading books they enjoy – including picture books – and pushed into reading educationally worthy books, then we are in danger of creating a generation of non-readers'. See P. Curtis, Ofsted orders schools to brush up their English teaching, *The Guardian* (19 June 2009).

9   The role teachers play in promoting reading for pleasure was emphasised by the Department for Education in their document entitled, *Research Evidence on Reading for Pleasure*, published in May 2012.

10 In 2011, following a tour of Charter Schools in the United States, the then secretary of state for education, Michael Gove, stated that a greater emphasis should be placed on children reading books written before 1900. See We must teach our children to love books again, *Daily Telegraph* (1 April 2011).

11 The quote comes from Philip Pullman.

12 'Think in ink' is a useful tip. For the last forty-three years, I have written things down that I want to remember. However, on this occasion I never noted down who made the comment.

13 This is a French proverb.

14 Tom Chivers argued that 'grammar Nazis' were killing the English language through their obsession with out-of-date rules in his article, Are 'grammar Nazis' ruining the English language? *Daily Telegraph* (19 March 2014). Many newspapers carried reports in 2016 which indicated that such people are likely to be introverted and disagreeable.

15 In 1962, Martin Joos identified five different language registers with which people needed familiarity if they were to be able to communicate verbally with confidence. His research was published in 'The five clocks' in the *International Journal of American Linguistics*.

16 The high stakes testing of pupils in schools may simply lead to high stakes cheating and also the loss of some of our best teachers. This argument is put forward by Steven D. Levitt and Stephen J. Dubner in *Freakonomics: A Rogue Economist Explores the Hidden Side of Everything* (London: Penguin, 2007).

17 In 2008, the Qualifications and Curriculum Authority identified six personal learning and thinking skills that pupils should develop through the national curriculum in *Personal, Learning and Thinking Skills: Supporting Successful Learners, Confident Individuals and Responsible Citizens*. Ref: QCA/08/3606.

18 In 2016, *The Guardian* and other newspapers reported on 'fresh humiliation' for the Department for Education when the answers to that year's spelling test for Key Stage 2 pupils were leaked on the internet. See R. Adams and S. Weale, Fresh humiliation as Sats answers published online for second time, *The Guardian* (10 May 2016).

Chapter 15: This way to the nuclear bunker and other secrets

1   For more information about inside out leadership, you could read my first book, *Leadership with a Moral Purpose: Turning Your School Inside Out* (2008). In short, an inside out leader has a deep understanding of the community they serve, coupled with deeply held beliefs about what the best primary education looks like. This is then used to create a compelling vision of a better future.

2   From The Analects of Confucius, Book IV.

3   This quotation is taken from the 2000 film, *The Dish*, which tells the story of how live footage of man's first steps on the moon was relayed from the Parkes Observatory in Australia.

4   Sir Alec Clegg, the former chief education officer for the West Riding of Yorkshire, recognised that many youngsters within the area

lacked confidence and the ability to use spoken English effectively. He placed great emphasis on creating the right experiences for the children in order to encourage them to speak and write with sensitivity.

5   See *The Excitement of Writing* (London: Chatto and Windus, 1963), p. 4.

6   This remark was reportedly made by the Estonian supermodel Carmen Kass.

7   The quote comes from a speech made by President Obama at a news conference with the Estonian president, Toomas Hendrik Ilves, in Tallinn, Estonia on 3 September 2014.

8   See L. West, Attention, men: don't be a creepy dude who pesters women in coffee shops and on the subway, *The Guardian* (21 October 2014).

9   I loved working alongside the pupils of St Bede's Catholic Primary School and I thank them for their contribution. I hope it reflects the sensitivity I have been describing.

10 This line comes from Zadie Smith's *White Teeth* (London: Hamish Hamilton, 2000), p. 541.

11 This is a collaborative piece from children at St Bede's Catholic Primary School.

12 See W. Mansell, R. Adams and P. Edwards, England schools: 10,000 pupils sidelined due to league-table pressures, *The Guardian* (21 January 2016).

13 In July 2015, *The Guardian* reported on the large numbers of children out of school as a result of exclusion. The children involved often had special educational needs, but schools were using exclusion procedures rather than having their examination statistics adversely affected. See R. Adams, English schools see first rise in exclusions in eight years, *The Guardian* (30 July 2015).

Chapter 16: *Real mathematics is based in the real world*

1   Conrad Wolfram, the British technician and businessman, argues that it is essential that computers are used in the teaching of mathematics because they are rather good at it. He was a significant figure in establishing the Estonian national curriculum.

2   If you would like to know more about Conrad Wolfram's exciting approaches to the teaching of mathematics, see his 2010 TED Talk, 'Teaching Kids Real Math with Computers' at: https://www.ted.com/talks/conrad_wolfram_teaching_kids_real_math_with_computers.

3   In 2016, the *Daily Telegraph* and *The Guardian* accused the then education secretary, Nicky Morgan, of presiding over a 'chaotic mess' when she appeared to explain the government's U-turn over their controversial plans to force every school in England to become an academy. See S. Weale, Nicky Morgan accused of creating chaotic mess despite academies U-turn, *The Guardian* (9 May 2016).

Chapter 17 : *Who wants to solve a quadratic equation anyway?*

1   Conrad Wolfram has called for a revolution in the way mathematics is taught in our schools. See C. Wolfram, The UK needs a revolution in the way maths is taught. Here's why …, *The Guardian* (23 February 2014).

2   Carol Dweck describes the importance of schools promoting a growth mindset in her book *Mindset: Changing the Way You Think to Fulfil Your Potential*, updated edn (London: Robinson, 2017).

3   Peter Mountstephen first introduced me to the notion of replacing the

title of 'head teacher' with 'head learner' during an inspirational presentation to the National Primary Trust in 2001.

4   Graham McPherson, also known as Suggs, is a writer, broadcaster, musician and entrepreneur who has performed to millions from the rooftop of Buckingham Palace. His school reports described him as lazy and incapable of improvement. See Suggs, *That Close* (London: Quercus, 2013), p. 56.

5   The song 'Baggy Trousers' appears on the 1980 album *Absolutely*.

6   In his book, *The Tipping Point*, Malcolm Gladwell describes that magic moment when an idea or innovation crosses a threshold and spreads like wildfire to become the new standard practice.

7   In August 2016, *The Guardian* produced evidence that the government's education policies relating to academies and free schools were leading to increased social segregation and this, in turn, was contributing to widening the poverty gap. See F. Millar, School reforms widen poverty gap, new research finds, *The Guardian* (2 August 2016).

Chapter 18: Without struggle there is no progress

1   In 2013, I had the privilege of hearing Sir Tim Brighouse addressing Lambeth head teachers

at their annual conference. He told them that 'the best head teachers have optimism beyond bounds'.

2   In *The Report of Her Majesty's Chief Inspector of Education, Children's Services and Skills 2013/14: Schools*, Sir Michael Wilshaw indicated that inspectors were actively going to seek out those effective schools that dared to be different, p. 18. The full report can be found at: https://www.gov.uk/government/publications/ofsted-annual-report-201314-schools-report.

3   The same messages were reiterated in Ofsted's revised *School Inspection Handbook* published in 2015, p. 41. The full document can be found at: https://www.gov.uk/government/publications/school-inspection-handbook-from-september-2015.

4   Susanna Rustin's article in *The Guardian* on 12 July 2016 outlined the work of a number of groups which had become tired of the government's education policies and were seeking to apply pressure which would lead to significant change.

5   See E. Harding, Parent protest today 'linked to teacher unions': campaigners accused of having a political agenda as thousands of children are set to miss school in demonstration against testing of six and seven-year-olds, *Daily Mail* (2 May 2016).

Bibliography

Adams, R. (2015). English schools see first rise in exclusions in eight years, *The Guardian* (30 July).

Adams, R. and Weale, S. (2016). Fresh humiliation as Sats answers published online for second time, *The Guardian* (10 May).

Adetunji, J. (2012). Michael Gove overruled experts to sell school playing fields, *The Guardian* (17 August).

Alexander, R. J. (2001). *Culture and Pedagogy: International Comparisons in Primary Education*. Malden, MA: Wiley-Blackwell.

Alexander, R. J. (ed.) (2009). *Children, Their World, Their Education: Final Report and Recommendations of the Cambridge Primary Review*. Abingdon and New York: Routledge.

Audit Commission (2008). *Value for Money in Schools – Literature and Data Review. Final Report*. Available at: https://eprints.soton.ac.uk/52002/1/Audit_Commission_-_Value_for_Money_in_Schools_-_final_report.pdf.

BBC (2011). Gove stresses 'facts' in school curriculum revamp, *BBC News* (20 January).

Bernstein, J. (1996). *Albert Einstein and the Frontiers of Physics*. New York: Oxford University Press.

Bew, P., Lord (2011). *Independent Review of Key Stage 2 Testing, Assessment and Accountability. Final Report*. London: Department for Education. Available at: https://www.gov.uk/government/publications/independent-review-of-key-stage-2-testing-assessment-and-accountability-final-report.

Board of Education (1935). *Handbook of Suggestions for Teachers*. London: HMSO.

Brighouse, T. and Woods, D. (eds) (2006). *Inspirations: A Collection of Commentaries and Quotations to Promote School Improvement*. London: Network Continuum Education.

Brown, L. (2014). Parents' fury after young girls who built den during holidays moved on by police who checked if they had Asbos, *Daily Mail* (21 April).

Calvin, M. (2012). The last word: Gove is selling children short, *The Independent* (4 November).

Campbell, A. (2015). *Winners and How They Succeed*. London: Arrow.

Casals, P. (1970). *Joys and Sorrows: Reflections*. New York: Simon & Schuster.

Chivers, T. (2014). Are 'grammar Nazis' ruining the English language? *Daily Telegraph* (19 March).

Chorley, M. (2013). 'Terribly formal' Michael Gove accused of running education department like *Are You Being Served?* (by one of his own ministers), *Daily Mail* (16 January).

Clark, C. (2013). *Children's and Young People's Reading in 2012: Findings from the 2012 National Literacy Trust's Annual Survey*. London: National Literacy Trust. Available at: http://www.files.eric.ed.gov/fulltext/ED560633.pdf.

Clark, C. and Foster, A. (2005). *Children's and Young People's Reading Habits and Preferences: The Who, What, Why, Where and When*. London:

National Literacy Trust. Available at: https://files.eric.ed.gov/fulltext/ED541603.pdf.

Clark, L. (2009). Teachers wear body armour to stop unruly pupils biting them, *Daily Mail* (15 April).

Clarke, C. (2003). Speech on secondary education at the conference: Collaborate, Create and Educate, London, 10 February 2003. Transcript available at: http://www.ukpol.co.uk/charles-clarke-2003-speech-on-secondary-education/.

Claxton, G. (2002). *Building Learning Power: Helping Young People to Become Better Learners*. Bristol: TLO Ltd.

Claxton, G. (2006). *Learning to Learn – The Fourth Generation: Making Sense of Personalised Learning*. Bristol: TLO Ltd.

Clegg, A. B. (1970). *The Excitement of Writing*. London: Chatto and Windus.

Collins, J. (2001). *Good to Great*. London: Random House.

Costa, A. L. (ed.) (2001). *Developing Minds: A Resource Book for Teaching Thinking*. Alexandria, VA: Association for Supervision & Curriculum Development.

Curtis, P. (2009). Ofsted orders schools to brush up their English teaching, *The Guardian* (19 June).

Daily Mail (2010). Call me Sir! Former troops to be recruited as teachers in crackdown on trendy schooling (24 November).

Department for Children, Schools and Families (2008). *Independent Review of the Primary Curriculum: Final Report* [Rose Review]. Nottingham: DCSF. Available at: http://www.educationengland.org.uk/documents/pdfs/2009-IRPC-final-report.pdf.

Department for Education (2012). *Research Evidence on Reading for Pleasure*. London: DfE. Available at: https://www.gov.uk/government/uploads/system/uploads/attachment_data/file/284286/reading_for_pleasure.pdf.

Department for Education and Skills (2003). *Excellence and Enjoyment: A Strategy for Primary Schools*. Norwich: DfES.

Department for Education and Skills (2004). *Excellence and Enjoyment: Learning and Teaching in the Primary Years. Professional Development Materials*. Norwich: DfES.

Department for Education and Skills (2005). *Excellence and Enjoyment: Social and Emotional Aspects of Learning*. Norwich: DfES.

Department of Education and Science (1959). *Primary Education: Suggestions for the Consideration of Teachers and Others Concerned with the Work of Primary Schools*. London: HMSO.

Department of Education and Science (1975). *A Language for Life* [Bullock Report]. London: HMSO.

Departmental Committee of the Board of Education (1921). *The Teaching of English in England* [Newbolt Report]. London: HMSO.

Dickens, C. (1995 [1854]). *Hard Times*. London: Penguin.

Dweck, C. (2017). *Mindset: Changing the Way You Think to Fulfil Your Potential*, updated edn. London: Robinson.

Dyson, J. (2013). Michael Gove overlooks engineering at his peril, *The Guardian* (15 April).

Fleming, N. and Baume, D. (2006). Learning styles again: VARKing up the right tree! *Educational Developments*, 7, 4–7.

Flood, A. (2013). Academics chastised for bad grammar in letter attacking Michael Gove, *The Guardian* (3 May).

Foster, P. (2016). Chris Packham: eat tadpoles to learn value of animal life, *Daily Telegraph* (29 May).

Fry, S. (2006). The future's in the past, *The Observer* (9 July).

Fullan, M. (2001). *Leading a Culture of Change*. San Francisco, CA: Jossey-Bass.

Gallo, C. (2014). *Talk Like TED: The 9 Public-Speaking Secrets of the World's Top Minds*. New York: St Martin's Press.

Gardner, H. (1983). *Frames of Mind: The Theory of Multiple Intelligences*. London: Heinemann.

Garner, R. (2013a). Crisis of confidence among civil servants in Gove's department, *The Independent* (23 September).

Garner, R. (2013b). How Rochdale Sixth Form College taught its teens to think bigger, *The Independent* (5 June).

Gladwell, M. (2002). *The Tipping Point: How Little Things Can Make a Big Difference*, new edn. London: Abacus Books.

Gove, M. (2011). We must teach our children to love books again, *Daily Telegraph* (1 April).

Gove, M. (2013). I refuse to surrender to the Marxist teachers hell-bent on destroying our schools: education secretary berates 'the new enemies of promise' for opposing his plans, *Daily Mail* (23 March).

Guardian, The (2014). Michael Gove urges 'traditional' punishments for school misbehaviour (2 February).

Gurney-Read, J. (2016). 'Unfair' primary school baseline assessments dropped as progress measure, *Daily Telegraph* (8 April).

Harding, E. (2016). Parent protest today 'linked to teacher unions': campaigners accused of having a political agenda as thousands of children are set to miss school in demonstration against testing of six and seven-year-olds, *Daily Mail* (2 May).

Helm, T. (2012). Jamie Oliver in blistering attack on Michael Gove over poor school diet, *The Guardian* (22 April).

Henley, J. (2010). Why our children need to get outside and engage with nature, *The Guardian* (16 August).

Higton, J., Leonardi, S., Richards, N., Choudhoury, A., Sofroniou, N. and Owen, D. (2017). *Teacher Workload Survey 2016. Research Report* (February). London: Department for Education.

Hilton, J. (1934). *Goodbye, Mr Chips*. London: Hodder & Stoughton.

Hope, C. (2013). One school playing field sold off every three weeks since Coalition was formed, *Daily Telegraph* (13 December).

Hurst, G. (2013). Pupils deserting arts subjects at GCSE 'because of Gove reforms', *The Times* (25 March).

Johnson, D. (2008). Many schools putting an end to child's play, *New York Times* (7 April).

Jones, O. (2014). *The Establishment: And How They Get Away With It*. London: Allen Lane.

Joos, M. (1962). The five clocks, *International Journal of American Linguistics*, 28(2), pt 5.

Judd, J. (1994). Patten offers education chief a libel settlement, *The Independent* (23 May).

Kennedy, M. (2014). *To Kill a Mockingbird* and *Of Mice and Men* axed as Gove orders more Brit lit, *The Guardian* (25 May).

Kotter, J. P. (1999). *What Leaders Really Do*. Boston, MA: Harvard Business School Press.

Lencioni, P. (2007). *The Three Signs of a Miserable Job: A Fable for Managers (and their Employees)*. San Francisco, CA: Jossey-Bass.

Levitt, S. D. and Dubner, S. J. (2007). *Freakonomics: A Rogue Economist Explores the Hidden Side of Everything*. London: Penguin.

Louv, R. (2010). *Last Child in the Woods: Saving Our Children from Nature-Deficit Disorder*. London: Atlantic Books.

Mansell, W. (2014). Free schools fail Ofsted inspections at much higher rate than state schools, *The Guardian* (29 April).

Mansell, W., Adams, R. and Edwards, P. (2016). England schools: 10,000 pupils sidelined due to league-table pressures, *The Guardian* (21 January).

Mansell, W. and Boffey, D. (2014). Academies run by 'superhead' received advance notice of Ofsted checks, *The Independent* (17 August).

Marsh, L. G. (1970). *Alongside the Child: Experiences in the Primary School*. London: A&C Black.

McCartney, P. (2012). John and I had a premonition of success, *Big Issue* (16 February).

Merrick, J. (2012). Gove and Leon chef dreamed up school meals deal over mojitos in Marrakech, *The Independent* (15 July).

Millar, F. (2016). School reforms widen poverty gap, new research finds, *The Guardian* (2 August).

Muir, H. (2013). Michael Gove's new GCSE exams leave pupils without a second chance, *The Guardian* (1 November).

Mullis, I. V. S., Martin, M. O., Kennedy, A. M. and Foy, P. (2006). *PIRLS 2006 International Report: IEA's Progress in International Reading Literacy Study in Primary Schools in 40 Countries*. Chestnut Hill, MA: TIMSS & PIRLS International Study Centre.

Nazarian, V. (2010). *The Perpetual Calendar of Inspiration: Old Wisdom for a New World*. Highgate Center, VT: Norilana Books.

Nelson, F. (2012). David Cameron's 'chumocracy' is no substitute for a political mission, *Daily Telegraph* (14 June).

Newman, J. R. (ed.) (1956). *The World of Mathematics*. New York: Simon & Schuster.

Ofsted (2005). *Primary National Strategy: An Evaluation of its Impact in Primary Schools 2004/05*. Available at: http://dera.ioe.ac.uk/5648/.

Ofsted (2008). *Learning Outside the Classroom: How Far Should You Go?* Available at: http://dera.ioe.ac.uk/9253/.

Ofsted (2009). *English at the Crossroads: An Evaluation of English in Primary and Secondary Schools, 2005/08*. Available at: http://dera.ioe.ac.uk/298/.

Ofsted (2012). Ofsted scraps 'satisfactory' judgement to help improve education [press release] (16 January). Available at: https://www.gov.uk/government/news/ofsted-scraps-satisfactory-judgement-to-help-improve-education.

Ofsted (2014). *The Report of Her Majesty's Chief Inspector of Education, Children's Services and Skills 2013/14: Schools*. Available at: https://www.gov.uk/government/publications/ofsted-annual-report-201314-schools-report.

Ofsted (2015a). *The Annual Report of Her Majesty's Chief Inspector of Education, Children's Services and Skills 2014/15: Education and Skills*. Available at: https://www.gov.uk/government/publications/ofsted-annual-report-201415-education-and-skills.

Ofsted (2015b). *School Inspection Handbook*. Available at: https://www.gov.uk/government/publications/school-inspection-handbook-from-september-2015.

Ofsted (2016). *The Annual Report of Her Majesty's Chief Inspector of Education, Children's Services and Skills 2015/16: Education and Skills*. Available at: https://www.gov.uk/government/publications/ofsted-annual-report-201516-education-early-years-and-skills.

Organisation for Economic Co-operation and Development (2002). *Reading for Change: Performance and Engagement Across Countries. Results from PISA 2000*. Available at: https://www.oecd.org/edu/school/programmeforinternationalstudentassessmentpisa/33690986.pdf.

Packham, C. (2016). *Fingers in the Sparkle Jar*. London: Ebury.

Paton, G. (2010). School pupils 'spend a year taking exams', *Daily Telegraph* (6 January).

Press Association (2012). Michael Gove defends £370,000 plan to send Bibles to schools, *The Guardian* (25 May).

Press Association (2014). Children's mental health menaced by 'unprecedented toxic climate', *The Guardian* (20 January).

Press Association (2016). Government accused over 'chaotic' education policy after Bill dropped, *Daily Mail* (28 October).

Qualifications and Curriculum Authority (2008). *Personal, Learning and Thinking Skills: Supporting Successful Learners, Confident Individuals and Responsible Citizens*. Ref: QCA/08/3606. London: QCA.

Ritchie, H. (2013). *English for Natives: Discover the Grammar You Don't Know You Know*. London: John Murray.

Robinson, K. (2010). Changing Education Paradigms, *TED.com* [video]. Available at: https://www.ted.com/talks/ken_robinson_changing_education_paradigms.

Rustin, S. (2016). Schools and the new parent power: this time, the fight is personal, *The Guardian* (12 July).

Ryan, W. (2008). *Leadership with a Moral Purpose: Turning Your School Inside Out*. Carmarthen: Independent Thinking Press.

Sainsbury, M. and Clarkson, R. (2008). *Attitudes to Reading at Ages Nine and Eleven: Full Report*. Slough: National Foundation for Educational Research.

Shepherd, J. (2012). Teachers don't know what stress is, says Ofsted chief, *The Guardian* (10 May).

Sinek, S. (2009). How Great Leaders Inspire Action, *TED.com* [video]. Available at: https://www.ted.com/talks/simon_sinek_how_great_leaders_inspire_action.

Smith, J. (2000). *The Learning Game: A Teacher's Inspirational Story*. London: Little, Brown.

Smith, Z. (2000). *White Teeth*. London: Hamish Hamilton.

Stanton, A. (2012). The Clues to a Great Story, *TED.com* [video]. Available at: https://www.ted.com/talks/andrew_stanton_the_clues_to_a_great_story.

Stewart, H. (2013). *The Happy Manifesto: Make Your Organization a Great Workplace*. London: Kogan Page.

Stewart, W. (2013). Ofsted faces legal action from inspectors, *TES* (5 April).

Strohmeyer, R. (2008). The 7 worst tech predictions of all time, *PCWorld* (31 December).

Suggs (2013). *That Close*. London: Quercus.

Thomson, A. and Sylvester, R. (2010). Gove unveils Tory plan for return to 'traditional' school lessons, *The Times* (6 March).

Usher, S. (ed.) (2013). *Letters of Note: Correspondence Deserving of a Wider Audience*. London: Canongate.

Vaughan, A. (2016). Boris Johnson accused of burying study linking pollution and deprived schools, *The Guardian* (17 May).

Velotta, R. N. (2013). A six-word slogan, and the marketing campaign to advertise it, cost Nevada $9 million, *Las Vegas Sun* (9 April).

Viner, B. (2012). The man who rejected the Beatles, *The Independent* (12 February).

Ward, H. (2012). All work and no play, *TES* (2 November).

Weale, S. (2016). Nicky Morgan accused of creating chaotic mess despite academies U-turn, *The Guardian* (9 May).

West, L. (2014). Attention, men: don't be a creepy dude who pesters women in coffee shops and on the subway, *The Guardian* (21 October).

Wilshaw, M. and Ofsted (2016). HMCI's monthly commentary: February 2016. Available at: https://www.gov.uk/government/speeches/hmcis-monthly-commentary-february-2016.

Wintour, P. (2012). Give Queen a new royal yacht for diamond jubilee, says Michael Gove, *The Guardian* (15 January).

Wolff, J. (2016). University research and the rise of academic bragging contests, *The Guardian* (17 May).

Wolfram, C. (2010). Teaching Kids Real Math with Computers, *TED.com* [video]. Available at: https://www.ted.com/talks/conrad_wolfram_teaching_kids_real_math_with_computers.

Wolfram, C. (2014). The UK needs a revolution in the way maths is taught. Here's why …, *The Guardian* (23 February).

Woodhead, L. (2007). *Shopping, Seduction & Mr Selfridge*. London: Profile Books.